The Samson Riddle

PUBLISHED WORKS

NOVELS
  Make Me an Offer
  A Kid for Two Farthings
  Laugh till you Cry
  My Old Man's a Dustman
  Cockatrice
  The Penguin Wolf Mankowitz

STORIES AND COLLECTIONS
  Majolika & Co. (juvenile)
  The Mendelman Fire
  Expresso Bongo
  The Peguin Wolf Mankowitz

CERAMIC HISTORY
  The Portland Vase
  Wedgwood
  Encyclopaedia of English Pottery and Porcelain

MUSICALS
  Expresso Bongo
  Make me an Offer
  Pickwick
  Israel 20

POETRY
  XII Poems

PLAYS
  Five One Act Plays
  The Bespoke Overcoat
  The Samson Riddle

THE
SAMSON RIDDLE

An Essay and a Play, with the text
of the original Story of Samson

WOLF MANKOWITZ

Drawings by Edward Delaney

VALLENTINE, MITCHELL — LONDON

First published by
by Vallentine, Mitchell & Co. Ltd.
67 Great Russell Street
London, WC1B 3BT

Copyright © Wolf Mankowitz 1972

The play is fully copyrighted and all applications for permission to perform it must be addressed to:
Margaret Ramsey Ltd.
12a Goodwins Court
London, WC2

The text of the Authorised Version of the Bible is Crown copyright, and the extracts used herein are reproduced by permission.

ISBN 0 853 03152 5

All rights reserved. No part of this publication may be reproduced, stored in a retrieval system, or transmitted in any form or by any means, electronic, mechanical, photocopying, recording, or otherwise, without the prior permission of Vallentine, Mitchell & Co. Ltd.

Printed and bound in Great Britain by
Tonbridge Printers Ltd., Peach Hall Works, Tonbridge, Kent

FOR MY FATHER

FOR MY FATHER

CONTENTS

The Essay   1

The Story of Samson   13

The Samson Riddle   23

This is the end of the matter;
all hath been heard:
fear God, and keep his Commandments;
for this is the whole duty of man.

ECCLESIASTES

The Essay

My father has, all his life, had an irresistible compulsion to accumulate books. Unlike most book-collectors, he then proceeds to read them with total concentration from beginning to end, as if searching for the secret of the world, which he knows must have been written down at some time, by someone. Always the book which could never exhaust his enquiring spirit has been the Old Testament; from him, I suppose, I acquired very early the habit of quite unreligious biblical study. I travel a great deal and have lived in many countries and the only book I ever carry with me is the Bible, (in the highly readable edition of Ernest Sutherland Bates*). I have pondered and searched *Ecclesiastes* 'on the shores of Asia and in the Edgware Road', and have always found in it the answer to (or at least an attitude towards) my current perplexity, but *Samson*, however often I read it, has always left me with one or another riddle.

I began writing *The Samson Riddle* in Jerusalem, continued it in Rome and London, and finished it four years later in Dublin – a lot of places and too much time for a fast-moving professional writer to spend on any piece. When it was finished I found that what had escaped my normally commercially committed pen was not so much a play as an enquiry in dialogue form, with a Samson who does not suffer from giantism but is a normal reasonably well-made man at twenty, and a little gone to fat at forty. For I found nothing in the original story to suggest that Samson had ever been anything but ordinary physically. He had simply been chosen by God for a special task and so, when the need arose, he was loaned special powers. The mighty strength was a divine investment: it was not dependent upon muscle development. Samson's contemporaries and the public since have been mass-hypnotized by his reputation as they were (and are) by any Emperor's new clothes.

By the general public Samson is only remembered as a huge

---

* *The Bible Designed To Be Read As Literature*, edited and arranged by Ernest Sutherland Bates (William Heinemann).

grotesquely comic idiot resembling Victor Mature, being betrayed by a fatal woman somewhere between Hedi Lamarr and Mata Hari, and revengefully pushing plaster columns down at Cinecitta in a low budget American-Italian spectacular. And yet, especially for a middle-aged Jewish artist, Samson embodies a number of fundamental riddles, and it was these riddles which began, one very hot afternoon in the then ruined building called the Khan in Jerusalem, to obsess me.

There is a condition much thought about today and known unamiably as 'the male menopause' which is particularly critical in artists and other men committed to the grandiose delusion of Purpose. In the late thirties it tends uneasily to manifest itself, a combination of fatigue, disillusionment and hope for a new, violent, and finally clear revelation. It is a malaise which seeks its resolution in strange countries, women, addictions, and affiliations. Men in their forties, their destinies already deeply committed, struggle to comprehend, twist, turn and shatter their lives in the attempt to break shackles of iron or gold, only, like Samson, to bend their heads finally to the forbidden question, offer the secret answer to the implacable enemy, suffer the inevitable blindness with deep relief, and go into seclusion to learn patience and await a clearer vision. It seems a unique and highly significant experience at the time, but is, in fact, a common concomitant of the onset of middle age and is, as I say, unflatteringly named by psychiatric doctors who have among their drugs many which may or may not successfully deal with endogenous or reactive depression. However, even after taking a pill the writing remains. The Book of the Judges contains this extraordinarily conceived and amazingly written story of Samson. It has haunted the imaginations and perplexed the intellects of artists through several thousand years of changing treatments for the problems of the male menopause; male delusions have risen and fallen in ruins about it while the story, like all great fables of the floundering of the human spirit in the drift of destiny, remains undamaged and unaltered. And the riddles it offers remain as essentially unanswerable as that of the Sphinx, for the true problem is, of course, in the answer. 'What goes on four legs, two legs, three legs?' It is the answer 'Man' which is the riddle.

Now as to Samson, many questions, all of them fundamental, arise. And many answers, all of them riddles, are offered. He is born late of a long barren mother and committed pre-natally to strange tabus and an obscure purpose. He must drink no wine, nor must his hair be cut, and he will 'begin' to lead his people out of bondage. But the restrictions are those of an indulgent society, and the bondage is a soft one. Samson's tribe is imprisoned by an idyllic agricultural life in a fertile country, and may not work iron. The masters are an indulgent sophisticated (perhaps) Cretan people who worship the fertile and the beautiful, intermarry with their bondsmen, come to their weddings, gamble and hunt with them, and forbid them to live in urban centres which are, anyway, cursed with the pollution of Dagonish worship, sacred prostitution, and beautiful idols. Not such a difficult bondage to live in, an affluent and permissive society which ought to be a bad place for producing violent revolutionary heroes. But Samson sees a gentile girl and decides for no great reason other than that 'she pleaseth me well', to marry her. No one objects very violently, because marrying-out goes on all the time in gently assimilationist societies. And so Samson's first major transgression against the tabus and commitments of his birth occurs, and the grinding mill of his God swings heavily into inexorable action.

To consider *Samson* first for what it will always be, an echo of Jewish culture, history and myth. Here is an account of a man raised from birth as a Nazarite – that is to say, he is committed to the fulfilment of a particular vow, he must 'begin to deliver Israel out of the hands of the Philistines'. Till such a vow was accomplished the Nazarite wore his hair uncut, eschewed wine, was not allowed to approach a dead body and foreswore women. Samson keeps his hair long and does not drink wine, but he takes honey from the dead body of a lion, is close to the dead he killed, and has a weakness for women, and gentile women at that. Three are mentioned: the Woman of Timnath, daughter of a Philistine vintner; the Harlot of Gaza, one of those sacred prostitutes who made Philistine places of worship appalling to the anti-erotic, anti-idolatrist Jewish puritans. And Delilah, the Woman of Sorek, desperate final passion of a middle-aged Judge, his unforgettable betrayer. So that Samson radically reneges against the Nazarite commitment. Yet struggle as he may to change the destiny to which he has been committed pre-natally, he cannot do so. He can affect the smoothness of its flow but the end designed by Samson's God will, one way or another, through one blunt instrument or another, through this or that mistake, by whatever meaningless events and obscure rituals, come to pass. Nothing happens against the will of God, and whether we understand it or not, find it loving or sensible or not, everything has a reason and the reason is beyond ours.

One night in New York I went to the midnight court of one of the last reigning Chassidic rabbis, to the Brooklyn school of the *Lubavitcher Rebbe*, to look for answers to some of the extraordinary riddles asked by the Samson story. Once you pass through the door of the Brooklyn *stebl* in the decaying ghetto, where the night is owned by the laughter of Negro militants and the morning wakes early to the praying of orthodox Jewish students, their hair and side-curls like Samson's, you enter the world of Isaac Bashevis Singer. In a nicotine-coloured room of books and fading photographs of sublime rabbinic ancestors the *Rebbe* interviews his followers throughout the night, judges their disagreements, solves their problems, gives guidance, and discusses the question of why Samson, a chronic defaulter, fulfilled his destiny. 'For Samson,' he explains, 'was no different, no stronger, no purer, no less wilful and no less blind than any other man. He was chosen to accomplish a divine purpose not for his heroic qualities but simply because he was chosen. Once chosen his human deviations could complicate the process but not change it. The Almighty leads – men must follow.' As the *Rebbe* talks my feeling grows that man is dispensable, that his species is largely wastage and his life has no meaning he can begin to understand. I say so, and the *Rebbe* explains that because this can happen man's best course is to follow, unquestioningly, the *Torah*. If he does so he will move with the Divine Purpose without ever having to ask or know what it is.

'As to wastage,' explains the *Rebbe*, 'one seed is fertilized and a hundred thousand are not lost but return into the system of which that solitary fertilisation is a part.' I feel that the difference between seeds and men is that each one of us is cursed and blessed with self-awareness. No other species is self-conscious, has an image of itself, continuously seeks identity. We are unable to enjoy so easily being the contribution of a seed to the nitrogen cycle. 'We are not important in the way in which we feel we are important, and we are important in a way in which we feel unimportant,' answers the *Rebbe*.

I ask two more questions about Samson. 'Why did he, knowing from experience that Delilah would betray him, nevertheless give her the secret of his strength?' The *Rebbe* explains that Samson was not responding to his reason but to the irresistible compulsion of his destiny. 'How often, when we do something unreasonable, do we truly express ourselves?' he undeniably observes.

My final question: 'Why did Delilah, with the world in her arms, betray it for silver?' Answer: 'Because she was a woman.'

It is nearly morning. Outside the door of the *Rebbe's* study the students wait, whispering like parchment, to ask me when I leave what he said. I am a Jewish alien and yet the *Rebbe* spent so long talking to me. Did he tell me the secret of the world? 'We talked about Samson,' I explained, and they are disappointed. 'Are you in trouble with a gentile woman?' asks one. 'We were talking about Samson,' I reply and walk into the dirty early morning street, more clear in my mind than I have been for a long time and, still not knowing the answers, less troubled by the abiding riddles.

To Gaza then I came, a few days after the Six Day War, to make a film about the emergent Israeli identity, and it seemed that the process Samson initiated was still in progress. The problem now – to secure the 'freedom' which results from the Samsonian way of being led out of bondage.

In Israel I became a purposive Jew, a sort of self-made time-bomb of the country which had resulted from the distant actions of the Judges. As Tel Aviv relaxed from the efforts of killing more Philistines in six days than they had in the twenty years before, I observed that the city was not exactly Nazarite in its disposition. The spirit of Samson was in the *nahals*, the settlements of young soldier-farmers, in the Army, and in the still ideologically pure minds of many of the leaders of the country. As world opinion, which had a few weeks before been poised on the edge of heartbroken sympathy for a small gallant about-to-be liquidated country, veered sickly into reverse, and, under the pressures of Russian, Arab, Left-Wing and merely traditionally anti-Semitic forces, began to project a ludicrously untrue image of Israel as a kind of Prussian-Jewish mutation, an aggressive little Semitic nazi with insane imperialist ambitions, it seemed possible that the commitment to fight the Philistines might last for ever. And, if so, could every phase of the battle be won? Supposing some future confrontation brought in Powers whose strength would require the direct intervention of *Jahveh* in order to assure Jewish victory – shouldn't the Jews prepare by reassuming ultra-orthodoxy? Weren't we required by our history to become a Nazarite people? In the event such a total conversion proved (as it always does) impossible, should we not expect the bloody consequences of a modern Samsonian syndrome – the continuous attrition of our own and the enemy's human and material resources? The Arabs announced at regular intervals that they were committed to *Jehad*; was the Jewish commitment also to an endless Holy War? In a country where we heard and used the word *Peace* a thousand times a day, was there never to be peace?

I searched through Israel for answers and found that the daily emergencies of life made it impossible to live there with doubt. The two basic Israeli responses were and had to be, 'There is no alternative' and 'Everything is possible, including the impossible'. At the Western Wall I put on *tefillim* and prayed to a pre-Christian God whose miracles were of a quality which might appal christianized Jews, but were the essence of our terrifying Jewish history. And so, in menaced Israel, my projects in shards about me, I felt a war-like kind of security – that which comes of thinking one knows the enemy and where he is. Back in London, the clamour of liberal christian socialist democratic voices sounded like the bedlam of a Philistine love-hate feast. I was born and raised in England but I knew finally that though England had not entirely made me, I had done nothing to make Israel and therefore had no permanent place there.

I now seemed able to read some of the runic marks on the Samsonian enigma. Samson's destiny had driven him to the place and moment when the lever of his forgotten strength could prize an unforgettable cause for vengeance out of his enemies. The Six Day War was such a lever. Israel could have, in twenty years, become a busy comfortable Levantine power, exchanging trade and culture with her neighbours, and, no doubt, the assimilating process would have blunted the historic memory of the Jews. But Israel was destined to remain Jewish; surrounded by a sea of implacable enemies the Jewish discussion of definition might continue but no one could talk himself out of being a Jew. And whatever pressures were upon Israeli Jews would be responded to by Jews elsewhere. The Samsonian definitive process is painful, but it works, and, because it has and does, another question throws its giant shadow across us.

Let me try to formulate that question. If Jews may be comfortably assimilated into other societies and peoples, and if this assimilation can, at the human level, show a pleasant return in living, why act against it? What, indeed, is the point of Jews remaining Jews either by their own efforts or by those of their enemies? Why must Samson pursue his painful individuation? Is there an end to the Jahvistic task? If Samson 'begins' the process, is it implied that there will be an *end* to it?

The dynamics of territorial affirmation are familiar and similar in all animal species. Political and physical reasons for grouping into territorially defined nationalities are equally unexclusive. The birds, the bees, lions and men all do it, although only the last kill their own kind for it. The pursuit of territorial identity, the redemption of a particular land after a two thousand year absence, the recreation of a national image and actuality, while being valuable, even essential to the political and social security of the Jews, cannot reasonably be considered to be the *end*. Jewish purpose, the sole reason why the Jews may have been *Chosen*, the primary Jewish contribution to the development of man, are the ethics and aesthetics of the Mosaic Code. And that Code, as Jewish nomadic history triumphantly demonstrates, is perfectly portable. In order to exist infuriatingly and challengingly Jewish Identity requires only commitment to the Decalogue. Given that commitment (even nominally) a disparate group of peoples of vastly varying and even contradictory supra-cultures can be fused into a national unit strong enough to create a country whenever the historical oportunity presents itself. The spark, then, lies not in the Land, but in the Law; it lies not in the world but in the Word. On that piece of Jewish Sinai rock the churches of the West have been built. Without it there is no western civilization. And yet, even with it, how few moments of civilized behaviour have there been during the three thousand years through which that Code has been promoted and protested, till now the whole western world with Judaeo-Christian principles sways on the edge of total self-annihilation. In such circumstances, if Jews are still 'chosen' what, one asks, are they chosen for? The answer must lie in terms of that highly portable, easily remembered, rarely observed Code. If the centres of civilization are destroyed in one holocaust, if Jerusalem itself with the last vestiges of the Temple and the national identity of the Jewish Israelis are all wiped out, somewhere, somehow, nomadic Jewish wanderers far from the centres of destruction will preserve the Code, and when ten of them meet in the desert of glass the civilizing process will begin again. It is not a prospect or a pattern to please us or make us feel secure in the pursuit of our vanities. But then happy endings are what children give to stories. Life demands only continuity, and perhaps the only safe assumption we may make about God's Nature is that it has a more consistent instinct for Life than we have, for our limited preoccupation is with our own lives. We cannot be pleased with playing the part of discarded seeds. And so it must have seemed to the men of Samson's time too, meaningless, cruel, impossibly burdensome, and endless.

So to the temptations of idolatry. To find relief from the labours of Samson in pursuit of the intentions of an obscure and non-human Divine Destiny, men invent gods they can understand, with passions like their own but magnified, and pleasures which they themselves can enjoy. Wine, wealth, power, death and sexual passion are the raw material of idols throughout man's history, so that since they are all monuments to human narcissism, there is comfort, relief and pleasure in their worship. But there is profound disillusionment as well, and revulsion and self-hatred; for being *of* man the idol must fail him in exactly the same ways that he fails himself. Hence the embargo 'Thou shalt have no other gods before Me', is a warning against the direly negative results of the worship by man of himself. Woman is equally fatal, whether she be worshipped as Earth Mother, or Female Principle, or Sacred Harlot, or Divine Madonna, or Heavenly Wife. Instead of elevating themselves to a parnassian playground man and woman should work equally together in the Task; otherwise they exploit, fight, and destroy one another; for to be used, even as a vehicle of worship, is to be made into an object, and all human beings, one way or another, sooner or later, revolt against such abuse. Thus Delilah resents being used by Samson as a vacation from his labours, a distractor of his strength from its unpleasurable purpose. She recognizes that his use of gentile women for uncommitted sexual relief is a denial of their reality as human beings. Consequently, she and they must all betray him, for their need to protest their own reality (which is a kind of love for God's creativity), must be greater than their 'love' for Samson. By such unconscious protest human beings fight whatever would deny the reality of their 'souls', their sense, that is, of their being subjects only to God. And when no other resistance is possible, they will simply lie down and quietly give up their ghosts.

Addiction is a kind of idol-worship and it is to release himself from it that Samson is compelled to reveal his secret, thus helping Delilah to help him to freedom by betrayal. Does that seem obscure? It isn't if we accept the end of the Samson story as intended; I mean the end as it relates to the history of the Jewish People, not the beautifully plotted story-elements in the original, the growing of the hair in the period of incarceration, and the return, after his prayer for revenge for the loss of his eyes, of his heroic strength. I believe that somehow or other a lot of Philistine nobles and priests did die when Samson died. I can see an ancient temple collapsing as a feast is in progress on its roof. I can believe that a blind hero with his confidence and strength suddenly returned, could dislodge an ancient key-stone. Since, however, Samson's heroic dismantling of the Temple of Dagon is the only element of his story which can be assumed to be known to everyone who recognizes his name, I decided to take the liberty of a Jewish artist to meddle with Jewish history.

In *The Samson Riddle* I postulate a situation in which the shorn and blinded Samson has become not only weak but impotent; I invent a Philistine priestly plot to assimilate the mythical virility of a defeated hero-god-leader into their people's strength, and win compensation for their losses. It may perhaps be argued against my variation that it removes the final decision for what happens from Samson, and that, in a heroic story, the hero must at least be the cause of the final victory or defeat. I made the variation not simply as an amusing and feasible fiction, but to show that whatever happened the end result would be the same. The recorders of history and those with perfect hind-sight make sure of that, and the instincts of the people for the inevitable, and the unbreakable sense of purpose that mothers have for their sons. I know very well that even if my account was certified truth they would have insisted upon the perfectly plotted, satisfyingly savagely horrific, and unforgettably apt original ending.

I salute the unknown writer of the original, and apologize for the deviations of my dialogue and action from his. He, pure Jew that he was, would, I hope, forgive me, in so far as I believe, as he did, that the task which Samson, the Jew, the Artist, Man, is committed to, is the witnessing of the Word as best he can. It is a lonely and frequently unhappy commitment: 'It is not thy duty to complete the task, but neither art thou free to desist from it.' We must do, to the extent of our ability, the work that comes to hand. Only then may we achieve the identity for which we are chosen, fulfilling ourselves, like Samson, in spite of our deviations So it is for Artists and Jews and Men.

'Where there are no men, be a Man.'

The Story of Samson*

* Original text from the Authorized Version of the Bible

The Story of Samson*

And the children of Israel did evil again in the sight of the Lord; and the Lord delivered them into the hand of the Philistines forty years.

And there was a certain man of Zorah, of the family of the Danites, whose name was Manoah; and his wife was barren, and bore not. And the angel of the Lord appeared unto the woman, and said unto her,

'Behold now, thou art barren, and bearest not: but thou shalt conceive, and bear a son. Now therefore beware, I pray thee, and drink not wine nor strong drink, and eat not any unclean thing: for, lo, thou shalt conceive, and bear a son; and no razor shall come on his head: for the child shall be a Nazarite unto God from the womb: and he shall begin to deliver Israel out of the hand of the Philistines.'

Then the woman came and told her husband, saying,

'A man of God came unto me, and his countenance was like the countenance of an angel of God, very terrible: but I asked him not whence he was, neither told he me his name: but he said unto me, "Behold, thou shalt conceive, and bear a son; and now drink no wine nor strong drink, neither eat any unclean thing: for the child shall be a Nazarite to God from the womb to the day of his death." '

Then Manoah intreated the Lord, and said, 'O my Lord, let the man of God which thou didst send come again unto us, and teach us what we shall do unto the child that shall be born.'

And God hearkened to the voice of Manoah; and the angel of God came again unto the woman as she sat in the field: but Manoah her husband was not with her. And the woman made haste, and ran, and showed her husband, and said unto him, 'Behold, the man hath appeared unto me, that came unto me the other day.'

And Manoah arose, and went after his wife, and came to the man, and said unto him, 'Art thou the man that spokest unto the woman?' And he said, 'I am.'

And Manoah said, 'Now let thy words come to pass. How shall we order the child, and how shall we do unto him?'

And the angel of the Lord said unto Manoah, 'Of all that I said unto the woman let her beware. She may not eat of any thing that cometh of the vine, neither let her drink wine or strong drink, nor eat any unclean thing: all that I commanded her let her observe.'

And Manoah said unto the angel of the Lord, 'I pray thee, let us detain thee, until we shall have made ready a kid for thee.'

And the angel of the Lord said unto Manoah, 'Though thou detain me, I will not eat of thy bread: and if thou wilt offer a burnt offering, thou must offer it unto the Lord.' For Manoah knew not that he was an angel of the Lord. And Manoah said unto the angel of the Lord, 'What is thy name, that when thy sayings come to pass we may do thee honour?'

And the angel of the Lord said unto him, 'Why askest thou thus after my name, seeing it is secret?'

So Manoah took a kid with a meat offering, and offered it upon a rock unto the Lord: and the angel did wonderously; and Manoah and his wife looked on. For it came to pass, when the flame went up toward heaven from off the altar, that the angel of the Lord ascended in the flame of the altar. And Manoah and his wife looked on it, and fell on their faces to the ground. But the angel of the Lord did no more appear to Manoah and to his wife. Then Manoah knew that he was an angel of the Lord.

And Manoah said unto his wife, 'We shall surely die, because we have seen God.'

But his wife said unto him, 'If the Lord were pleased to kill us, he would not have received a burnt offering and a meat offering at our hands, neither would he have showed us all these things, nor would as at this time have told us such things as these.'

And the woman bore a son, and called his name Samson: and the child grew, and the Lord blessed him. And the Spirit of the Lord began to move him at times in the camp of Dan between Zorah and Eshtaol.

And Samson went down to Timnath, and saw a woman in Timnath of the daughters of the Philistines. And he came up, and told his father and his mother, and said,

'I have seen a woman in Timnath of the daughters of the

Philistines: now therefore get her for me to wife.'

Then his father and his mother said unto him,

'Is there never a woman among the daughters of thy brethren, or among all my people that thou goest to take a wife of the uncircumcised Philistines?'

And Samson said unto his father, 'Get her for me; for she pleaseth me well.'

But his father and his mother knew not that it was of the Lord, that he sought an occasion against the Philistines: for at that time the Philistines had dominion over Israel.

Then went Samson down, and his father and his mother, to Timnath, and came to the vineyards of Timnath: and, behold, a young lion roared against him. And the Spirit of the Lord came mightily upon him, and he rent him as he would have rent a kid, and he had nothing in his hand: but he told not his father or his mother what he had done. And he went down, and talked with the woman; and she pleased Samson well.

And after a time he returned to take her, and he turned aside to see the carcase of the lion: and behold, there was a swarm of bees and honey in the carcase of the lion. And he took thereof in his hands, and went on eating, and came to his father and mother, and he gave them, and they did eat: but he told not them that he had taken the honey out of the carcase of the lion.

So his father went down unto the woman: and Samson made there a feast; for so used the young men to do. And it came to pass, when they saw him, that they brought thirty companions to be with him. And Samson said unto them,

'I will now put forth a riddle unto you: if ye can certainly declare it me within the seven days of the feast, and find it out, then I will give you thirty sheets and thirty changes of garments: but if ye cannot declare it me, then shall ye give me thirty sheets and thirty changes of garments.'

And they said unto him, 'Put forth thy riddle, that we may hear it.'

And he said unto them,

> 'Out of the eater came forth meat,
> And out of the strong came forth sweetness.'

And they could not in three days expound the riddle. And it came to pass on the seventh day that they said unto Samson's wife, 'Entice thy husband, that he may declare unto us the riddle, lest we burn thee and thy father's house with fire: have ye called us to take that we have? is it not so?'

And Samson's wife wept before him, and said, 'Thou dost but hate me, and lovest me not: thou hast put forth a riddle unto the children of my people, and hast not told it me.'

And he said unto her, 'Behold, I have not told it my father nor my mother, and shall I tell it thee?'

And she wept before him the seven days, while their feast lasted: and it came to pass on the seventh day that he told her, because she lay sore upon him: and she told the riddle to the children of her people. And the men of the city said unto him on the seventh day before the sun went down,

> 'What is sweeter than honey?
> And what is stronger than a lion?'

And he said unto them,

> 'If ye had not plowed with my heifer,
> Ye had not found out my riddle.'

And the Spirit of the Lord came upon him, and he went down to Ashkelon, and slew thirty men of them, and took their spoil, and gave change of garments unto them which expounded the riddle. And his anger was kindled, and he went up to his father's house. But Samson's wife was given to his companion, whom he had used as his friend. But it came to pass within a while after, in the time of wheat harvest, that Samson visited his wife with a kid; and he said, 'I will go in to my wife into the chamber.' But her father would not suffer him to go in. And her father said,

'I verily thought that thou hadst utterly hated her; therefore I gave her to thy companion: is not her younger sister fairer than she? take her, I pray thee, instead of her.'

And Samson said concerning them, 'Now shall I be more blameless than the Philistines, though I do them a displeasure?'

And Samson went and caught three hundred foxes, and took firebrands, and turned tail to tail, and put a firebrand in the midst between two tails. And when he had set the brands on fire, he let them go into the standing corn of the Philistines, and burnt up both the shocks, and also the standing corn, with the vineyards and olives.

Then the Philistines said, 'Who hath done this?'

And they answered, 'Samson, the son-in-law of the Timnite, because he had taken his wife, and given her to his companion.'

And the Philistines came up, and burnt her and her father with fire.

And Samson said unto them, 'Though ye have done this, yet will I be avenged of you, and after that I will cease.'

And he smote them hip and thigh with a great slaughter: and he went down and dwelt in the top of the rock Etam.

Then the Philistines went up, and pitched in Judah, and spread themselves in Lehi. And the men of Judah said, 'Why are ye come up against us?'

And they answered, 'To bind Samson are we come up, to do to him as he hath done to us.'

Then three thousand men of Judah went to the top of the rock Etam, and said to Samson, 'Knowest thou not that the Philistines are rulers over us? what is this that thou hast done unto us?'

And he said unto them, 'As they did unto me, so have I done unto them.'

And they said unto him, 'We are come down to bind thee that we may deliver thee into the hand of the Philistines.'

And Samson said unto them, 'Swear unto me that ye will not fall upon me yourselves.'

And they spoke unto him, saying, 'No; but we will bind thee fast, and deliver thee into their hand: but surely we will not kill thee.'

And they bound him with two new cords, and brought him up from the rock. And when he came unto Lehi, the Philistines shouted against him: and the Spirit of the Lord came mightily upon him, and the cords that were upon his arms became as flax that was burnt with fire, and his bands loosed from off his hands. And he found a new jawbone of an ass, and put forth his hand, and took it, and slew a thousand men therewith. And Samson said,

> *'With the jawbone of an ass, heaps upon heaps,*
> *With the jaw of an ass have I slain a thousand men.'*

And it came to pass, when he had made an end of speaking, that he cast away the jawbone out of his hand, and called that place Ramath-lehi. And he was sore athirst, and called on the Lord, and said,

'Thou hast given this great deliverance into the hand of thy servant: and now shall I die for thirst, and fall into the hand of the uncircumcized?'

But God clove a hollow place that was in the jaw, and there came water thereout; and when he had drunk, his spirit came again, and he revived: wherefore he called the name thereof Enhakkore, which is in Lehi unto this day. And he judged Israel in the days of the Philistines twenty years.

Then went Samson to Gaza, and saw there a harlot, and went in unto her. And it was told the Gazites, saying, 'Samson is come hither.' And they compassed him in, and laid wait for him all night in the gate of the city, and were quiet all the night, saying, 'In the morning, when it is day, we shall kill him.'

And Samson lay till midnight, and arose at midnight, and took the doors of the gate of the city, and the two posts, and went away with them, bar and all, and put them upon his shoulders, and carried them up to the top of a hill that is before Hebron.

And it came to pass afterward that he loved a woman in the valley of Sorek, whose name was Delilah. And the lords of the Philistines came up unto her, and said unto her,

'Entice him, and see wherein his great strength lieth, and by what means we may prevail against him, that we may bind him to afflict him: and we will give thee every one of us eleven hundred pieces of silver.'

And Delilah said to Samson, 'Tell me, I pray thee, wherein thy great strength lieth, and wherewith thou mightest be bound to afflict thee.'

And Samson said unto her, 'If they bind me with seven green withes that were never dried, then shall I be weak, and be as another man.'

Then the lords of the Philistines brought up to her seven green withes which had not been dried, and she bound him with them. Now there were men lying in wait, abiding with her in the chamber. And she said unto him,

'The Philistines be upon thee, Samson.' And he broke the withes, as a thread of tow is broken when it toucheth the fire. So his strength was not known. And Delilah said unto Samson, 'Behold, thou has mocked me, and told me lies: now tell me, I pray thee, wherewith thou mightest be bound.'

And he said unto her, 'If they bind me fast with new ropes that never were occupied, then shall I be weak, and be as another man.'

Delilah therefore took new ropes, and bound him therewith, and said unto him, 'The Philistines be upon thee, Samson.' And there were liers in wait abiding in the chamber. And he broke them from off his arms like a thread.

And Delilah said unto Samson, 'Hitherto thou hast mocked me, and told me lies: tell me wherewith thou mightest be bound.'

And he said unto her, 'If thou weavest the seven locks of my head with the web.'

And she fastened it with the pin, and said unto him, 'The Philistines be upon thee, Samson.'

And he awaked out of his sleep, and went away with the pin of the beam, and with the web. And she said unto him,

'How canst thou say, "I love thee", when thine heart is not with me? thou hast mocked me these three times, and hast not told me wherein thy great strength lieth.'

And it came to pass, when she pressed him daily with her words, and urged him, so that his soul was vexed unto death, that he told her all his heart, and said unto her, 'There hath not come a razor upon mine head; for I have been a Nazarite unto God from my mother's womb: if I be shaven, then my strength will go from me, and I shall become weak, and be like any other man.'

And when Delilah saw that he had told her all his heart, she sent and called for the lords of the Philistines, saying, 'Come up this once, for he hath showed me all his heart.'

Then the lords of the Philistines came up unto her, and brought money in their hand. And she made him sleep upon her knees; and she called for a man, and she caused him to shave off the seven locks of his head; and she began to afflict him, and his strength went from him. And she said,

'The Philistines be upon thee, Samson.' And he awoke out of his sleep, and said, 'I will go out as at other times before, and shake myself.' And he wist not that the Lord was departed from him.

But the Philistines took him, and put out his eyes, and brought him down to Gaza, and bound him with fetters of brass; and he did grind in the prison house. Howbeit the hair of his head began to grow again after he was shaven.

Then the lords of the Philistines gathered them together for to offer a great sacrifice unto Dagon their god, and to rejoice: for they said, 'Our god hath delivered Samson our enemy into our hand.'

And when the people saw him, they praised their god: for they said, 'Our god hath delivered into our hands our enemy, and the destroyer of our country, which slew many of us.'

And it came to pass, when their hearts were merry, that they said, 'Call for Samson, that he may make us sport.'

And they called for Samson out of the prison house; and he made them sport: and they set him between the pillars. And Samson said unto the lad that held him by the hand, 'Suffer me that I may feel the pillars whereupon the house standeth, that I may lean upon them.'

Now the house was full of men and women; and all the lords of the Philistines were there; and there were upon the roof about three thousand men and women that beheld while Samson made sport. And Samson called unto the Lord, and said, 'O Lord God, remember me, I pray thee, and strengthen me, I pray thee, only this once, O God, that I may be at once avenged of the Philistines for my two eyes.'

And Samson took hold of the two middle pillars upon which the house stood, and on which it was borne up, of the one with his right hand, and of the other with his left. And Samson said, 'Let me die with the Philistines.'

And he bowed himself with all his might; and the house fell upon the lords, and upon all the people that were therein. So the dead which he slew at his death were more than they which he slew in his life. Then his brethren and all the house of his father came down, and took him, and brought him up, and buried him between Zorah and Eshtaol in the burying place of Manoah his father. And he judged Israel twenty years.

THE SAMSON RIDDLE

A PLAY

The Samson Riddle was first produced as a reading at the Gate Theatre on March 19, 1972, as part of the Dublin Drama Festival. The principal parts were as follows:

MANOAH	Hilton Edwards
DELILAH / BRIDE	Susannah York
SAMSON'S MOTHER	Miriam Karlin
SAMSON	Hugh Millais
VINTNER / BARBER / SCRIBE	Noel Purcell
RABBI	Liam Miller
ZOAB	Alun Owen

PRODUCTION NOTE

The Samson Riddle is designed to be produced on the barest possible stage with the minimum essential props and within three principal acting areas, between which movement is paralleled by cross-fading lights.

The costumes should be simple caftans, white, black or striped, in silk or linen, depending upon the status of the characters.

The set should be a system of simple blocks and platforms at various levels, which are used as seats, tables, steps, etc., as required.

The music should be sparsely used and of an electronic nature, so as to build up to a large sound effect in the penultimate scene to simulate the destruction of the Temple, during which special lighting effects are required.

The dialogue-style is deliberately eclectic and utilizes Yiddish rhythms, but should be played naturally without any strong over-accentuation of any kind. In the passages printed in bold type (which are quotations from the original story) the *vatic* effect should be momentarily under-scored by lighting and a single musical chord, the lines being delivered at a slower pace and in a classical key.

It is not necessary to have a large cast. Apart from the Principals, the cameos and trios of Suitors, Elders and Priests may be doubled as convenient.

ACT ONE

SCENE 1 MANOAH'S HOUSE

SAMSON'S MOTHER, a dignified, young middle-aged woman, is praying before a hermaphroditic effigy.

MOTHER (*intensively*) You came to me, Angel, when I worked in the fields and you said, 'Behold thou art barren but thou shalt conceive and bear a son.' And where is he now Angel? We both know where he is. It's not my fault. I did as you told me. 'Drink not wine nor strong drink and eat not any unclean thing while you are pregnant,' you said, 'and you shall bear a son.' And I did, and I did. 'And no razor shall touch his hair, for the child shall be a Nazarite unto God from the womb.' I did it. Didn't I do it? And where is he now? Where is my Nazarite son? 'And he shall begin to deliver Israel out of the hand of the Philistines,' you promised. That little boy with long curls will begin to deliver us. And now he is a man with hair of gold and red, like rays of the sun, and where is that man, the hero of his people, that Nazarite pure from the womb? (*She suddenly bursts out, unable to contain herself.*) Whoring with the filthy bitches of Timnath, that's where he is! Damn all lying promises from men and angels! (*She lashes out at the effigy which falls to the stone floor and breaks. After a shocked moment she starts to pick up the pieces.*) I'm sorry. I'm sorry. I didn't mean it. You can't know a mother's feelings. Excuse me, forgive me, Angel. (*The latter part of her prayer has been observed by her husband,* MANOAH, *who has entered quietly and watched her, shaking his head deprecatingly. Now he joins her and on his*

	hands and knees starts to help her pick up the broken pieces of the effigy.)
MANOAH	(*gently*) Why do you talk to these idols, woman? You talk to them, you beg them, you scream at them, you shout at them, you kiss them, you break them. Figures of clay. What for?
MOTHER	I don't need any help from you.
MANOAH	But what is the sense of it, woman?
MOTHER	Sense? What's the sense of any of it?
MANOAH	(*sighs*) How can we know the sense of the Lord?
MOTHER	And that's you, isn't it? That's just how you are. No questions, just grovel and let it happen. Get up off your knees if you're a man.
MANOAH	I'm helping you, aren't I?
MOTHER	I don't need your help. Where's the head? Have you got the head?
	(MANOAH *gets up and drops onto the floor the pieces of the idol he holds.*)
MANOAH	Clay, shaped by a potter in Gaza to something that is neither man nor woman.
MOTHER	(*defiantly*) My angel. (*She picks up the pieces he has thrown down protectively, then sighs as she studies them.*) This is too badly gone to repair. Never mind. (*She drops the pieces onto the floor, and gets up.*) I'll get another one. Maybe the blacksmith can make one in copper. Then it won't break.
MANOAH	So you'll have a copper angel, you can make copper prayers to it. What's to eat?
MOTHER	There's honey-cake and milk on the table.
MANOAH	So I'll eat. Shearing the sheep is hard work. The wool is thin this year. The price won't be so good. (*He sits down and eats and drinks. The* MOTHER *has picked up a broom and sweeps up the broken fragments of the idol.*)
MOTHER	Sheep, wool, prices, eat. What about Samson? Where is he?
MANOAH	You, I and the Angel know where he is. He's in Timnath.
MOTHER	And you eat – you drink – you shear the sheep.

MANOAH	(*mildly*) And you worship an idol.
MOTHER	That's different. Are you comparing me with those Philistine whores?
MANOAH	(*still mild*) Come woman – they're not all whores. The girl Samson goes to see is a fifteen-year-old virgin.
MOTHER	Any one of their fifteen-year-old virgins can become a sacred prostitute any time of the day or night.
MANOAH	Alright, but her father's wine is the best in Timnath and, furthermore, we have a treaty of friendship with his people.
MOTHER	Friendship! We are slaves! We are conquered! They do with us what they please.
MANOAH	So what do they do? They conquered our tribe twenty years ago and since that time there has been no war. We live in peace, they live in peace, our boys marry their girls, their nobles marry our women. The only thing is they won't let us work from iron. So what! Better they should keep their secret weapons. For me a wood plough is still good enough.
MOTHER	(*defiantly*) Why shouldn't we work from iron? With iron we would destroy them.
MANOAH	That's why. Look – it all makes for peace. The flocks grow. We worship in our way, they worship in their way. The ways even get a little bit mixed up – as you yourself know.
MOTHER	I know what I know. Don't you tell me what I know.
MANOAH	(*shrugs*) Alright. I'll finish my breakfast and get back to the sheep.
MOTHER	That you can do but what will you do about Samson?
MANOAH	(*with slight anger for the first time*) What will I do? I'll tell you what. What you've always permitted me to do about Samson. Nothing. He's a child of prophecy, you always told me. He's watched over by an Angel, you said. He has to be brought up this way and that way. He has to

	have that ridiculous long hair. These are all your ideas, woman. I spoke to the rabbi* about it, you know what he said?
MOTHER	I don't care what he said.
MANOAH	I'll tell you. He said, 'What can I say? Samson is a typical product of a permissive upbringing. Stubborn, wayward, wilful, tricky, strong-headed, wrong-headed, and certain to come to a bad end.' That's what the rabbi thinks. And me? I've got sheep to shear. (*He gets up and picks up his shears.*)
MOTHER	(*appealingly*) But Manoah, tell me.
MANOAH	(*irritably*) What? What?
MOTHER	What are we going to do about Samson?
MANOAH	He's coming now. Ask him yourself.
MOTHER	Don't you dare go. You stay. You face out something for once in your life.
MANOAH	There's still more than half the flock to shear.
MOTHER	You'll stay or I'll never speak to you again. (*For a moment* MANOAH *considers the possibility, as if it wouldn't be so terrible if she didn't. Then he shrugs and sighs.*)
MANOAH	So I'll stay. (*He puts down his shears resignedly.* SAMSON *enters. While being well-built, he is in no way a giant, or strongman. His strength comes from God not from muscles. He is in his twenties, his hair red-gold in long wild ringlets. He carries over his shoulder the skin of a lion fresh and bloody, which he throws down on the floor.*)
SAMSON	(*uncertainly*) Father and Mother. Uh – good morning, isn't it?
MOTHER	(*with forced calm*) So it's a beautiful morning. Good. Where have you been all night?
SAMSON	I brought you a lion's skin to keep you warm this winter. (MANOAH *goes over to the skin and examines it.*)
MOTHER	Rugs we've got. Rugs we're not short of.

* There were, of course, no rabbis in the time of Samson. One of several anachronisms produced by the Yiddish flavour of Manoah and Samson's mother.

MANOAH	It is! It's another enormous mountain lion. You killed it yourself?
SAMSON	With my bare hands.
MANOAH	You see, woman? This is marvellous for the sheep-raising. Samson has killed so many mountain lions with his bare hands, we hardly lose a lamb anymore. And you know what the percentage of losses to mountain lions used to be?
MOTHER	Don't bother me with economics. (*To* SAMSON) Where were you all night?
SAMSON	What? I'm starving. What's to eat? (*He drains a beaker of milk on the table and starts to eat honey cake voraciously.*)
MANOAH	(*admiringly*) With his bare hands. How he does it on such a diet, I cannot understand.
MOTHER	You? You could never understand. Like everyone else your mind is too simple. But I believe. I know that if God wills it a midget can make a nonsense from a giant. My Samson doesn't have to be a monster to have a monstrous strength. He was an underweight baby and already I knew. He just has to live clean and be a good Jew. Samson, you're deaf all of a sudden? I asked where were you all night.
SAMSON	(*mouth full*) Where? In Timnath, where else?
MOTHER	All night?
SAMSON	(*swallowing*) Why not? We went hunting this morning. I made a bet with the Philistines.
MOTHER	So – gambling!
MANOAH	There's nothing that says a Nazarite boy can't gamble, woman.
MOTHER	And drinking perhaps you were?
SAMSON	You know I don't drink. I let them drink. That way the next day they won't hunt so well. (*He laughs.* MANOAH *also laughs.*)
MANOAH	He's no fool, our boy.
MOTHER	And women? What about women?
MANOAH	What do you mean, what about women? He's a strong, normal Jewish boy. What do you want?
MOTHER	Were there women, Samson?

SAMSON	Certainly there were women.
MOTHER	(*triumphantly*) Philistine women!
SAMSON	A few Jewish women too. You know, wives of some of the Philistines.
MANOAH	Yes, that's another thing. This very Timnath girl's mother is Jewish.
MOTHER	(*coldly*) I was not aware that we were discussing a particular Timnath girl. Are we discussing something in particular, because if so, as Samson's mother, I think I am entitled to know. (MANOAH *and* SAMSON *exchange a glance*.)
MANOAH	(*resignedly*) You'd better tell her, Samson.
SAMSON	(*evasively*) Tell her? Tell her what?
MANOAH	With mountain lions a hero, but with his own mother – alright, I'll tell her. Samson wants to marry the Timnath girl. (*The* MOTHER *is dumbstruck for a moment. Then she puts her hands to her head and covers her eyes.*)
MOTHER	No, never. It's not possible. They can't do this to me, they wouldn't. (SAMSON *looks at her with bleak helplessness for a moment then:*)
SAMSON	I'll help you with the sheep, father.
MANOAH	Good idea.
SAMSON	Let's go. (*Their threatened exit brings the* MOTHER *together rapidly*.)
MOTHER	Where do you think you're going?
MANOAH	Samson's helping me finish the sheep.
MOTHER	Not until I've had my say, he's not.
MANOAH	But the sun is reaching its height. Who can shear sheep in the heat of the day?
MOTHER	Let the sheep drop dead. You listen to me. (*to* SAMSON) **Is there never a woman among the daughters of thy brethren or among all thy people that thou must take a wife of the uncircumsized Philistines?***

* Whenever the actual Biblical language is used a special tone of destiny enters the scene. The characters are for the moment possessed, and such quotations are played, as it were, in parenthesis to the body of the piece.

SAMSON	(*coldly*) **Get her for me; for she pleaseth me well.** (*There is a moment of silence as the* MOTHER *takes in the absolute finality of* SAMSON'S *decision.*)
MOTHER	(*brokenly*) That's all you have to say to me, my son?
SAMSON	That's all. (*to* MANOAH) Let us to work, father.
MANOAH	The wool is thin this year.
SAMSON	The drought last winter.
MANOAH	Water – that's the whole problem of this damned country, with water it would flow with milk and honey – (*They exit. The* MOTHER *stands agonized for a moment and then she drops to her knees.*)
MOTHER	(*praying*) A man came unto me and his countenance was like the countenance of an Angel of God – very terrible. And he said unto me... 'Behold thou shalt conceive and bear a son, and he shall be a Nazarite to God from the womb to the day of his death and he shall begin to deliver Israel out of the hand of the Philistines.'

SCENE 2 AT THE FOLDS

Sometime later; SAMSON and MANOAH have finished the sheep shearing.

SAMSON	That's the last one. You're right, the wool is thin this year.
MANOAH	The drought is the curse of this damned country. My God, Samson, we finished the whole flock and it's still daylight. That strength of yours is no joke, my boy.
SAMSON	I wanted to finish early.
MANOAH	Uh-huh?
SAMSON	I told her father you would meet with him today.
MANOAH	You're really serious about marrying the girl?
SAMSON	I am.
MANOAH	But Samson – why marry? We could pay her father concubine money instead of bride money, You get your way, you send her back when you're tired of her, all it does is increase her value as a bride, your mother won't be upset, and there's no harm done to anyone. Why marry the girl Samson? (SAMSON *doesn't answer*.) I mean – what's so special about a fifteen-year-old Philistine girl?
SAMSON	She has thirty important Philistine suitors.
MANOAH	So she's a beautiful girl. When you've finished with her the suitors can bid for her. Why marry?
SAMSON	(*uneasily*) I know, I know. She giggles and wants to dance all the time yet I must marry her.
MANOAH	Look, Samson – we've all been in love a dozen times. There's nothing about love that marriage can't cure. But it's so drastic, son.
SAMSON	I must, that's all.
MANOAH	This is a very unnatural feeling for a young man. Can you describe it a little more?
SAMSON	To tell you the truth, father, the Voice tells me.

MANOAH	(*dismayed*) Oh no! Not that Voice again. You promised me you didn't hear the Voice anymore.
SAMSON	Well, it's true – I don't hear it as often as I used to. But sometimes it still speaks.
MANOAH	Look, it makes no sense, my son. I can understand it when the Voice was saying to you as a small boy 'Guard the law', 'Build yourself up for the struggle against the enemy', 'Lead a clean life' and all that sort of stuff. This is what holy voices are supposed to say to a young fellow. But 'Marry a fifteen-year-old Philistine girl who giggles and dances' – is that something for a holy voice to say to a carefully brought-up Jewish boy?
SAMSON	What can I do? That's the message.
MANOAH	Listen, Samson – I know from my talks with the rabbi that the human mind is a very strange business. You're sure you're reading the message properly?
SAMSON	Father, there's no argument about this. The message comes through in pure Biblical Hebrew.
MANOAH	(*sighs*) Well, it's just another mystery, that's all. A holy voice sends you a ridiculous message in a language which hasn't even been fully invented yet.
SAMSON	I know it has something to do with my career. This marriage will affect my whole future.
MANOAH	You're damned right it will. For a boy as promising as you to whom so many of the younger Jews look up with respect, a lot of them even saying they are going to vote you the next Judge, this decision can be a calamity. It's a terrible political mistake, Samson. Do me a favour. Let's offer her father double the concubine price and forget the marriage. (SAMSON *stands as if listening to something. His father looks at him hopefully. Then* SAMSON *shakes his head and sighs.*)
SAMSON	Sorry, father. The message is quite clear. I have to marry the girl.

MANOAH	You have to marry her, eh?
SAMSON	(*resignedly*) I have to. But somehow I don't think it's going to be a straightforward, normal marriage like you and mother.
MANOAH	Please God. Alright then. Let's go and make the deal. As a matter of fact, with the wool so poor this year, even the bride price I am going to have to argue about a little bit.
SAMSON	The girl and her father are mad for me. She won't be expensive.
MANOAH	Well, that's a blessing anyway. We'd better go. It's a fair walk to Timnath.
SAMSON	On the way I'll show you the carcase of the mountain lion I killed.
MANOAH	I'd like to see it. You know killing all these mountain lions has got you a wonderful reputation. (*he sighs*) It's a pity you have to lose it for a giggling girl with St. Vitus dance. Still, that's how we men are when it comes to girls.
SAMSON	I told you, it's not the girl – it's the Voice.
MANOAH	Alright, it's the Voice, it's the Voice. But I still say that's how we men are when it comes to girls.

SCENE 3 THE HOUSE OF THE TIMNATH VINTNER

PHILISTINE SUITORS, identically dressed in white silk robes, sit around at the end of the feast to celebrate Samson's marriage to the Vintner's daughter.
SAMSON and MANOAH sit to either side of the VINTNER. In a separate area are the WOMEN of the Vintner's family around the WOMAN OF TIMNATH, a fifteen-year-old girl dressed in bridal clothes. Her face is veiled.
The VINTNER is a typically affable, heavily-built, middle-aged merchant farmer – very Jewish – with a strong accent.

VINTNER Drink, drink, my friends. Enjoy, enjoy. This is – I say it without false modesty – the best wine of the best vineyard in all our beautiful country of Philistia, including the occupied territories of our dear friends and neighbours with whom today we pledge yet another bond of friendship and peace. To you thirty noble, distinguished, handsome suitors who have complimented my house by paying your addresses to my beautiful daughter, I say thank you from the bottom of my heart. I only wish that I had what it takes to give you a daughter apiece. But at my age, even on my wine, not even the Harlot of Gaza herself can do very much for me. Mind you – I still have my moments – don't I, Mothers? I get no complaints from my seven wives. But gentlemen, enough is enough and I am sorry that with the best will in the world, I cannot satisfy you all. I mean you thirty distinguished suitors – not you seven happy, happy wives. So here we are together, friends. My old friend Manoah – a great fellow, even if he is a Jew – and my marvellous, fantastic, heroic new son-in-law, Samson. I cannot tell you what it means to a father when one of his seventeen favourite daughters makes such a

	marriage. Also friends, do not let us overlook the political significance of the occasion. By marrying this beautiful girl of mine....
BRIDE	(*giggling*) Oh, Daddy, stop....
VINTNER	... Samson forges a bond of association between our two peoples which, we all know, from twenty years of happy living together we do not really need. But on the other hand – it doesn't do any harm to know that an instrument like Samson is on our side. So now, before the happy couple retire ... to check over their wedding presents, let me thank my old friend Manoah for the marvellous gift of two pedigree rams. One is already looking after my ewes, and the other ... (*he indicates* SAMSON) ... soon will be. (*laughter*) Let me also thank Samson himself for bringing as a present some of the best honey I have ever tasted. I did not know that you were a great bee-man as well as a great sheep-man, Manoah, but that honey, that was something special. And now I am going to stop boring you all with the ramblings of a happy father and ask my distinguished son-in-law Samson to say to you a few words before he disappears for the ritual seven days with my lovely daughter whom I give to him with the deep feeling in my heart that, if I may coin a phrase, I am not losing a daughter but gaining a champion for our people. (SAMSON *stands up. There is an expectant silence as he looks around and seems unable to find anything to say.*)
MANOAH	(*whispers loudly*) Say something, Samson. This is an occasion.
VINTNER	(*to* MANOAH) The boy is overwhelmed, no?
MANOAH	(*urgently to* SAMSON) Samson, speak. Speak! (SAMSON *makes noises, but no clear words emerge from his mouth.*)
1ST SUITOR	Look at him! He's so dumb!
BRIDE	With a body like that who needs to talk?

MANOAH (*loud whisper*) Please Samson, something, anything. (*embarrassed to* VINTNER) The boy is overwhelmed, you understand. You have made such a marvellous occasion here. We are a simple people. The lad's not used to it.

VINTNER (*put out*) I understand. But something he should say.

SAMSON (*declaims suddenly*)
Out of the eater came forth meat, And out of the strong came forth sweetness.
(*There is silence for a moment and then puzzlement.*)

VINTNER (*to* MANOAH) What did he say?

MANOAH (*hurriedly*) It's a riddle, friend. Among our people great occasions are commemorated with magical riddles.

VINTNER Oy! What a people! (*to* SAMSON) Alright, son-in-law – it's a riddle, friends. Say again, Samson.

SAMSON **Out of the eater came forth meat, And out of the strong came forth sweetness.**

VINTNER Beautiful. But what does it mean?

MANOAH (*quickly*) You see, it means like if you are strong you can also be a very sweet person. No, Samson?

SAMSON (*quietly*)
If ye can certainly declare the answer to me within the seven days of the feast, then I will give to you thirty Philistines thirty sheets and thirty changes of garments. But if ye cannot declare it to me then shall ye give me thirty sheets and thirty changes of garments.

VINTNER (*delighted*) I understand! What a boy! What a gambler! He knows our people love a gamble. What do you say, lads? Do you accept the bet of my brilliant son-in-law?

SUITORS Why not? We'll gamble on anything! It's easy. What was it? Out of the strong came forth meat. No, no. . . . Etc.,

VINTNER Very good, Samson. My thirty noble friends will answer your riddle. (*aside to* MANOAH) If they

	can, which frankly I don't believe, because what sense does it make?
MANOAH	(*aside*) The sense that it makes, dear friend, is that Samson is going to bring to your beautiful daughter a marvellous trousseau.
VINTNER	He's a clever boy.
MANOAH	(*proudly*) Not clever, friend, inspired.
VINTNER	Hup! Let the dancing begin. (*A small group of Philistine musicians starts to tune up. The* BRIDE *leaps to her feet.*)
BRIDE	Mother of Dagon, I thought they'd never finish. (*she calls to the* SUITORS) I'm going to dance with all of you for the last time. Who's first?
1ST SUITOR	As the first of all your suitors, bride, I claim the right of the first dance.
2ND SUITOR	Since when was there any such right?
1ST SUITOR	Since now. (*He draws his dagger.*)
BRIDE	(*petulantly*) No fighting on my wedding day. I won't dance with anyone who kills anyone. (*The* MUSICIANS *break into a jerky Philistine number.*)
BRIDE	(*to* 1ST SUITOR) Come on then. (*As they dance. . . .*) I love this song. It's the rage of Gaza. (*The* BRIDE *and the* 1ST SUITOR *as they dance are isolated from the party.*) I suppose you often go to the Temple of Gaza?
1ST SUITOR	My family are hereditary oil-bearers.
BRIDE	I've never been.
1ST SUITOR	You never will, now.
BRIDE	I will if I want to.
1ST SUITOR	A good Jewish wife in the Temple of Dagon – please!
BRIDE	I can go into any temple I want.
1ST SUITOR	That's what you think.
BRIDE	I can and I will.
1ST SUITOR	You just don't know what being a Jewish wife means.
BRIDE	I do so. My mother's Jewish.
1ST SUITOR	Not for the Jews she isn't any more.
BRIDE	She always goes when Daddy visits the sacred prostitute. She loves it.

1ST SUITOR	But do you ever see the wives of any Jews there?
BRIDE	What difference does that make?
1ST SUITOR	You'll find out.
BRIDE	You're just jealous.
1ST SUITOR	Of that big idiot?
BRIDE	If he's such an idiot, answer his riddle.
1ST SUITOR	I will.
BRIDE	So give me the answer.
1ST SUITOR	No, baby bride. You give me the answer.
BRIDE	(*puzzled*) What do you mean?
1ST SUITOR	(*after a beat, and in a sinister tone*) **Entice thy husband that he may declare unto us the riddle.**
BRIDE	Why should I?
1ST SUITOR	**Entice him lest we burn thee and thy father's house with fire.**
BRIDE	You wouldn't dare.
1ST SUITOR	We would, baby bride, we would.
BRIDE	(*shocked*) Burn me and my father's house?
1ST SUITOR	With fire. (*The music dies away. The* BRIDE *stares at the* 1ST SUITOR, *frightened.*)
BRIDE	(*quietly*) **I will entice him.**

SCENE 4   THE MARRIAGE CHAMBER

The BRIDE drifts from the dancing area, leaving the SUITOR behind her. The lights reveal SAMSON waiting, combing his hair thoughtfully. She starts to undress.
As she takes off her veil she looks towards him expectantly. He ignores her.

BRIDE　　　　I've taken off my veil.
SAMSON　　　Oh yes.
BRIDE　　　　My veil.
SAMSON　　　Yes.
BRIDE　　　　It's off.
SAMSON　　　Yes.
　　　　　　　(*The* BRIDE *bursts into tears*.)
BRIDE　　　　I've never been so insulted in my life.
SAMSON　　　What's the matter?
BRIDE　　　　You didn't dance with me.
SAMSON　　　I don't dance. You danced with everybody else. What are you crying about?
BRIDE　　　　(*wails*) You're my husband and you don't even want to look at me the first time I take off my veil!
SAMSON　　　Of course I want to look at you. Come here.
BRIDE　　　　No.
SAMSON　　　Please come to me.
BRIDE　　　　I don't want to.
SAMSON　　　I want to see your face.
BRIDE　　　　No you don't.
SAMSON　　　I do.
BRIDE　　　　I don't know why you married me if you don't want to look at my face.
SAMSON　　　I tell you I do.
BRIDE　　　　Then why didn't you look at me when I took off

	my veil? There's thirty noble Philistine suitors would knife one another to death for such a sight. (*she starts to sob again*) And you just go on combing your ridiculous hair.
SAMSON	Look, my dear –
BRIDE	(*with sudden realization*) Oh Mother of Dagon! No! –
SAMSON	(*puzzled*) What?
BRIDE	You're a pederast!
SAMSON	I? (*he laughs*) Ask them in Gaza!
BRIDE	Oh, they were right when they said 'Have fun in the vineyards with them, but never, never marry one. They're all perverts.' They were right!
SAMSON	Look, you dirty-minded little whore –
BRIDE	'Oh no,' I said, 'I've known a few of those Jewish boys and there's nothing like that about them,' I said. More fool me! Oh woe is me – woe – nothing but woe! (*She sinks down on to a bed of sheepskins.*) **Thou dost hate me and lovest me not.**
SAMSON	Look, let's get a few things clear. I don't hate you, and I am not one of your Philistine temple sodomites. It's just that I've a lot on my mind at present.
BRIDE	(*sobs*) Oh woe is me – woe – nothing but woe. (SAMSON *kneels down beside her on the bed and tries to comfort her.*)
SAMSON	Come now. This is our wedding night. Will you cry it away? (*The* BRIDE *pulls away from him like a wild-cat.*)
BRIDE	Don't you touch me. You long-haired thing – you big, stupid Jew.
SAMSON	(*discomfited by the girl's venom*) Look here – even a Philistine woman is supposed to respect her husband.
BRIDE	Why should I respect a man who doesn't love me?
SAMSON	I do. I do.
BRIDE	Don't lie to me.

SAMSON	Why would I marry you if I didn't love you?
BRIDE	Some filthy Jewish plot, I suppose. Oh you're so cunning your lot!
SAMSON	A marriage couch is not the place for an anti-Semitic demonstration. Is it?
BRIDE	Look at him. Big, strong, beautiful and absolutely useless to a woman.
SAMSON	(*annoyed*) You fork-tongued little Philistine bitch! (*He smashes her across the face with the back of his hand. She collapses onto the bed. The* BRIDE *looks up at him, a new light dawning in her eyes.*)
BRIDE	You do love me!
SAMSON	Love? Love is the talk of girls and the action of men.
BRIDE	But –
SAMSON	(*brutally*) Shut your mouth and open your legs.
BRIDE	(*meekly*) Yes, husband.

SCENE 5 THE TENT OF THE SUITORS

Three of the SUITORS are sitting huddled together gambling with dice in a desultory sort of way as they discuss SAMSON'S riddle.

2ND SUITOR — Out of the eater came forth sweetness.
3RD SUITOR — Meat, meat, you fool.
2ND SUITOR — Meat, I mean. And out of the strong came forth weakness.
3RD SUITOR — Sweetness, you idiot, sweetness.
2ND SUITOR — Alright, sweetness. Can somebody please tell me why we are sitting around like a bunch of bloody rabbis arguing the ins and outs of some stupid Jewish conundrum?
3RD SUITOR — Because if we don't work it out it's going to cost us a lot of silk, that's why.
2ND SUITOR — So – out of the strong came forth meat. What does that mean?
3ND SUITOR — From the strong came forth the sweetness, imbecile.
2ND SUITOR — Oh yeh. It's from the eater came forth the meat.
3ND SUITOR — I think I've got the answer. Out of the eater came forth meat. Right?
2ND SUITOR — Right.
3RD SUITOR — So that means the eater who eats meat is himself for somebody else, meat. Right?
2ND SUITOR — Oh – great solution I'm sure, like steaks eat steaks. Where does that get us?
3RD SUITOR — And out of the strong came forth sweetness. Well, that's got to mean something that's strong can also be like – very nice.
2ND SUITOR — Oh please. I mean, let's smoke or drink or something. This is just wasting the whole night.
3RD SUITOR — So we enjoy ourselves and it'll cost us a fortune. Is that clever?
2ND SUITOR — No, look – why not? I mean there's a lot of very strong things that if you tame them you can keep

	them around the place. Like a fox. I knew a fellow had a tame fox –
3RD SUITOR	What's so strong about a fox?
2ND SUITOR	Alright then – a bull is strong. But a bull can be very, very sweet. My uncle has a bull. He's just like one of the family.
3RD SUITOR	(*laughs*) The Vintner has a bull and he *is* one of the family. (*The* FIRST SUITOR *who has been listening to all this now speaks.*)
1ST SUITOR	Relax, gentlemen. I have the solution.
2ND SUITOR	So tell us, tell us.
1ST SUITOR	When I know, you shall know.
2ND SUITOR	What does that mean?
3RD SUITOR	That means that like the rest of us, he doesn't know.
1ST SUITOR	Not yet – but I will – and you will – and that arrogant circus strong man will lose this game.
2ND SUITOR	I don't know what we're all getting so concerned about anyway. I mean, a silk robe and a bed-sheet – I've lost more than that on a turn of the dice before. It's not such a big deal – and we had a marvellous dinner.
3RD SUITOR	Listen, it's not the price – it's the principle.
1ST SUITOR	Exactly. If we allow these Jews to ridicule us there will be no end to their effrontery.
2ND SUITOR	Oh come on – they're nice people. We've lived with them a long time now. We never have any trouble.
1ST SUITOR	You forget that before we conquered them they raided our territories, captured our women, burnt our temples, ridiculed our gods. Don't be fooled by this peace and quiet between our peoples. Give them an inch, they'll take a yard. Give them a yard, they'll take a mile. Give them ten miles and they'll take Gaza itself.
3RD SUITOR	(*uncomfortably*) I don't like this kind of talk. I'd rather lose the bet. What the hell. Anyone for dice?
1ST SUITOR	That's right, gentlemen. Play on. Relax. Enjoy yourselves. We've won.

2ND SUITOR   (*rolling dice*) I'm glad you think so. Alright. Here they roll. Come on, babies, show Daddy three beautiful phallic symbols. Huh! (*The game continues.*)

SCENE 6   THE MARRIAGE CHAMBER

SAMSON lies on the couch staring at the ceiling.
The BRIDE is curled up, turned away from him, huddled under a sheepskin.

SAMSON	What was that? (*The* BRIDE *throws the sheepskins off her head.*)
BRIDE	I said, that was some marriage night.
SAMSON	We'll improve. You move around like a snake.
BRIDE	That's how they taught me at the temple. Our priestesses know more about this kind of thing than your old fogies will ever know.
SAMSON	Why make such a big thing of it?
BRIDE	(*indignantly*) Why? I'll tell you why? Because I'm supposed to have a climax, that's why. What do you think the other girls in my clan would say if they knew on my marriage night I didn't have a climax?
SAMSON	You know too much about sex. It's not healthy.
BRIDE	You are, I suppose.
SAMSON	I haven't had any complaints before from your women.
BRIDE	Of course you didn't. Our girls are too polite, that's why. Also with us it's a religious duty before marriage. We're not looking for pleasure. But after marriage – what the hell else is there in it for us? Babies?
SAMSON	For a fifteen-year-old girl your ideas are deplorable.
BRIDE	I'm a wife, and a wife can say what she likes. Furthermore, she is entitled to a climax.
SAMSON	Let's forget it now. I'm tired. (*The* BRIDE *jumps up from the bed, absolutely furious.*)
BRIDE	You're tired! What do you think you've done? Killed a thousand mountain lions or something?

	I mean – really – if that tires you I can see I'm in for a marvellous married life.
SAMSON	Can't you understand? I've had lot on my mind the past few days.
BRIDE	Maybe it's on your mind, big man, but it certainly isn't anywhere else.
SAMSON	I have special problems.
BRIDE	You can say that again.
SAMSON	Anyway, I understood from your father that you were an innocent, sweet little virgin.
BRIDE	So?
SAMSON	So where's the evidence?
BRIDE	(*with great dignity*) I am a certified technical virgin.
SAMSON	What's that?
BRIDE	It means that since the age of twelve I have only consorted with men on a purely religious basis. And I have a certificate to prove it.
SAMSON	So you're not a virgin.
BRIDE	I'm a virgin to marriage, aren't I? And so far as I'm concerned, even after marriage I'm still a virgin.
SAMSON	(*indignantly*) But you've been with other men – God knows how many.
BRIDE	(*coolly*) I know exactly how many. How could I pass my exams if I didn't know exactly how many? Oh, it's a waste of time talking to you. You're just an ignorant Jewish shepherd brute. You know nothing about the refinements of life.
SAMSON	And you do, of course.
BRIDE	I graduated second in my class for Courtship Technique, third for Deviations and first in Massage, Cretan style.
SAMSON	So?
BRIDE	So what? (*suddenly distracted*) Your latissima dorsi are huge.
SAMSON	Teach me something.
BRIDE	(*weakening*) I'm not going to teach you anything until I'm sure you love me. Why should I?
SAMSON	I love you. I must love you.

BRIDE	No.
SAMSON	I'm insane with love for you. I hear voices.
BRIDE	I don't believe you.
SAMSON	Look, how can I prove I love you?
BRIDE	Well, you failed the first test – miserably.
SAMSON	Forget it, please. I was worried. And also the place is unfamiliar.
BRIDE	(*sagely*) That's true. In sexual congress unfamiliar circumstances are a prime source of anxiety. That's one of our lessons. Maybe you do have a little excuse.
SAMSON	You see?
BRIDE	But only a little one. I still don't know yet that you love me.
SAMSON	So how do I prove it?
BRIDE	If a lover tells his beloved a secret known only to himself, this is considered conclusive proof of love and will create a climate congenial to successful connection.
SAMSON	(*shrugs*) Alright – but what secret can I tell you? (*The* BRIDE *now approaches* SAMSON *very seductively, and twines herself around him like a slim little serpent. She looks up into his eyes, kisses his face, descending to his lips, and then after a long lingering embrace which leaves him rocking, speaks:*)
BRIDE	**Thou hast put forth a riddle unto the children of my people and hast not told it me.**
SAMSON	**Behold, I have not told it my father nor my mother, and shall I tell it thee?** (*The* BRIDE *withdraws from him.*)
BRIDE	There – you see – you don't love me. You impotent, stupid, sexless, unloving Jewish brute.
SAMSON	(*hurriedly*) Alright then. I'll tell you the answer to the riddle. (*The* BRIDE *approaches him again and puts her arms about him.*)
BRIDE	(*whispers*) My lovely, virile, gorgeous, enormous, sweet and loving Jewish brute. Tell me, tell me!

SCENE 7 TENT OF THE SUITORS

The three SUITORS stand waiting as SAMSON approaches.

1ST SUITOR	**What is sweeter than honey? And what is stronger than a lion?** (SAMSON *stops amazed*.)
SAMSON	What did you say?
1ST SUITOR	'What is sweeter than honey? And what is stronger than a lion?' What do *you* say?
SAMSON	(*after a pause*) **I say that if ye had not ploughed with my heifer, ye had not found out my riddle.** (*The* 1ST SUITOR *smiles and the other* SUITORS *look at one another with smiles of satisfaction*.)
1ST SUITOR	When will you pay, friend? (SAMSON *suppresses his tremendous anger*.)
SAMSON	When I collect, friend.
1ST SUITOR	When shall we know, friend?
SAMSON	Friend – you will know. (*The* SUITORS *start to disperse. The* 2ND SUITOR *starts to speak to* SAMSON.)
2ND SUITOR	Look, Samson, women are neither Jewish nor Philistine but a separate nationality, why fall out over them? (SAMSON *stares at him*.) Oh, never mind! (*He exits after the others.* SAMSON *stands for a few moments, his head bent as if listening. He shakes his head as if to clear it and hear better.* MANOAH *enters and watches him*.)
SAMSON	(*aside*) I do not hear you clearly. No. I do not hear. Your voice is lost in the roar of the fountain of fire which burns in my blood.
MANOAH	Why so much anger for so small a cause? The girl is kin to them. They threatened her. Frightened, she spoke. It's an expensive joke, Samson, that's all.

SAMSON	Whose joke?
MANOAH	Your joke – your riddle – these tricks go against oneself sometimes. It's the luck of the game.
SAMSON	Whose game?
MANOAH	The game, the game we play to pass the time and keep the mind from worse things. Thirty lengths of silk cost maybe a flock and a half of sheep, but it's not the end of the world. Come.
SAMSON	But this game – this joke – this trick which starts with an engagement in Timnath, proceeds to an encounter with a lion, continues with a nest of bees, forms itself into a riddle and discovers in its answer betrayal and fury – whose joke is this?
MANOAH	Forget it. Tonight we'll sleep. Tomorrow I'll ask the rabbi. Why do you hesitate? What do you hear? (SAMSON *is listening attentively.*)
SAMSON	I must go to Ashkelon.
MANOAH	To Ashkelon? Why? In Ashkelon the Philistines are laughing tonight over your defeat. Why look for trouble? Better to pay up and forget it.
SAMSON	I go to Ashkelon – to pay.
MANOAH	And forget it?
SAMSON	The jokes of Jahveh are unforgettable. (*He exits.*)
MANOAH	Please, Samson... (*he sighs*) I suppose he is my son, but every day I see less resemblance. (*Shaking his head sadly,* MANOAH *exits.*)

SCENE 8   THE HOUSE OF THE TIMNATH VINTNER

The VINTNER is in a high state of excited anxiety. He paces back and forth, shouting.

VINTNER : Bring wine. Has she come back yet?
WOMAN : She'll be back soon.
VINTNER : I never heard of such a thing. Such a barbarian! Such a peasant animal I should welcome into my house! Oh Dagon, forgive me for my heart is too big, my nature too generous, my mind too unquestioning. What can they do to me for this?
WOMAN : What can they do to you? It's not your concern.
VINTNER : He's kin, isn't he? This bloody monster is our kin! Oh the shame of it! The danger of it! Where is that idiot girl? There aren't enough noble suitors of our own people for her taste. She has to have a Jewish monster to bring trouble on my house. (*he shouts*) Where is she?
WOMAN : She's coming. She's coming.
VINTNER : She can't even go and get me the scribe without making a whole argument out of it. (*falsetto*) 'I'm a married woman now. I don't have to run errands.' (*reverts to normal voice*) What a marriage! What a calamity!
WOMAN : What an excitement! Maybe it's not even true.
VINTNER : Not true! In Ashkelon I saw the robes myself. Crimson they were with the blood of his victims, thirty fine Philistine boys, boys from Ashkelon. In a great pile he threw their robes down, steaming with blood, before the thirty noble suitors. 'Now I have paid,' he said. Thirty fine young men of our people lose their lives, so that he may make his bloody jokes. My God – I must find out my legal position. Where is that slut of a daughter of mine?

WOMAN	She's here. She's here. With the Scribe (*The* BRIDE *enters with an elderly Philistine* SCRIBE.)
WOMAN	(*to* BRIDE) What took you so long?
BRIDE	You expect me to run like a child? I'm a married woman.
VINTNER	You married woman, get out! (*He slaps her hard across the backside and she exits noisily.*)
WOMAN	It's not the girl's fault.
VINTNER	(*screams*) Get out, all of you. Damned stupid women! Where's the wine?
WOMAN	It's there, it's there. (*She indicates the table, and exits.*)
VINTNER	(*to* SCRIBE) Take some wine. (*The* SCRIBE *goes to take wine.*) No, don't. We haven't got time. You heard?
SCRIBE	Your son-in-law is proclaimed throughout the country as the murderer of thirty fine young men in Ashkelon. He's a strong boy. I'm so out of breath. I'll take a little. (*He pours himself a little wine.*)
VINTNER	So you heard – so tell me.
SCRIBE	It's a beautiful wine.
VINTNER	I sent for a lawyer, not a drinking companion. (*He snatches the goblet away from the* SCRIBE.) What is my legal position?
SCRIBE	Well – he *is* kin.
VINTNER	Thank you. This I know. To be told this I don't have to pay a Scribe a barrel of good wine every year.
SCRIBE	On the other hand. Supposing the marriage was never consummated –
VINTNER	(*indignantly*) What do you mean, never consummated? You think I would give my favourite daughter to an impotent?
SCRIBE	We all know it was consummated – but if it hadn't been, then in our law it would be no marriage.
VINTNER	(*getting the point*) It was never consummated. My daughter will swear it.
SCRIBE	In such a case the woman would be eligible for

	another husband, and then from a purely legal point of view I don't see how you could be considered the kin of Samson.
VINTNER	Me, the kin of that alien devil? The very suggestion is an insult. Draw up a marriage contract immediately.
SCRIBE	With whom?
VINTNER	With one of the thirty good, honest Philistine suitors.
SCRIBE	Alright. But which one?
VINTNER	Questions, questions. Pick any suitor.
SCRIBE	And the bride price?
VINTNER	Forget it. In this case, I'm paying. (SAMSON *enters from behind the* VINTNER. *The* SCRIBE *sees him*.) Why are you standing like you've been struck dumb? (SAMSON *advances into the eyeline of the* VINTNER. *His clothes are bloodied*.)
VINTNER	(*nervously*) Oh Samson, I'm glad to see you. (*to* SCRIBE) Go now and do as we have agreed.
SCRIBE	I go, I go. (*He hurries out*.)
SAMSON	I would go in to my wife.
VINTNER	But –
SAMSON	What?
VINTNER	Look, I thought you hated her, so I gave her to one of our own boys. But look, Samson, I'll give your father back the whole bride price, plus a flock of first-class ewes. And I'll stand the loss of the wedding, which didn't cost buttons. Fair, Samson?
SAMSON	(*sighs deeply*) **Now shall I be more blameless than the Philistines.** (*He turns to go*.)
VINTNER	Samson –
SAMSON	(*with savage coldness*) Yes, Philistine. (*pleading*) What will you do now, Sir? You won't do something ridiculous? After all –

SAMSON   What I must do, I will do. (*The* VINTNER *collapses utterly.*)
VINTNER Dagon, protect us poor ordinary people. What will this raving lunatic and his insane God do next?

SCENE 9 MANOAH'S HOUSE

It is night. A small lamp burns.
MANOAH is at the table, eating. SAMSON'S MOTHER is serving him.

MOTHER	So where is Samson?
MANOAH	I told you before. He's catching foxes.
MOTHER	(*angrily*) Stop making ridiculous excuses. Where is he?
MANOAH	He's catching foxes.
MOTHER	If you must lie for the boy, think of a clever lie.
MANOAH	(*wearily*) Look. For the past three days he didn't go to the sheep folds. I saw him this morning on the hill. I said to him 'Where have you been?' He said to me he's been catching foxes.
MOTHER	My son the furrier! By you men, a woman is expected to believe anything.
MANOAH	I'll take some more of the goat cheese.
MOTHER	You've had all there is. What will he do with the foxes?
MANOAH	What will he do? How do I know what he will do? The Philistines have two regiments of soldiers looking for him and he is suddenly an animal lover! What do I know about Samson?
MOTHER	He's really catching foxes?
MANOAH	He says he needs three hundred.
MOTHER	Why so many?
MANOAH	Why not? At least it's good for the flocks. The foxes take a lot of kids. You know – maybe after that unfortunate business in Ashkelon he feels he should atone with a little social service. That could be it. (*Through* MANOAH'S *speech a flickering red light from flames in the fields outside starts to illuminate the room.*)
MOTHER	(*worriedly*) The boy is getting so I don't know him any more. That marriage was a terrible

MANOAH	mistake. I always said so. The whole thing was a shock to his system. What's this light? It was a shock to the whole social system. There are always incidents among the young but thirty Philistines killed in cold blood – it's not so easy to overlook. (*The* MOTHER *crosses to the door.*)
MOTHER	What's all the light? (MANOAH *now notices the increasing red light from the spreading fires in the countryside. He gets up startled.*)
MANOAH	What is it?
MOTHER	(*alarmed*) There's flames spreading everywhere! It's a fire! (*The light from the flames increases.* MANOAH *stands beside her at the door looking out towards the back of the auditorium.*)
MANOAH	The flames are spreading like red quicksilver – here and there, low to the ground. I never saw such a fire before.
MOTHER	The sheep! Go to the folds!
MANOAH	The fire doesn't move that way. It moves towards Timnath.
MOTHER	But the wind blows in the opposite direction.
MANOAH	Yes. The fire moves against the wind! This I never saw before.
MOTHER	It's a miracle!
MANOAH	What are you talking about – a miracle? What good does a fire bring anyone? I'll go to the sheep. (*He hurries out. She watches the fire fascinated.*)
MOTHER	(*fervently*) Fire of the Angel, burn the Philistines. Burn them. Burn them.

SCENE 10 THE HOUSE OF THE TIMNATH VINTNER

The same flames are being watched by the terrified VINTNER and his family. But the flames are brighter and stronger from their angle.

VINTNER	(*shouts*) The flames are coming closer!
BRIDE	But the wind – the wind blows the other way.
WOMAN	The fire runs across the ground like snakes, like scorpions.
VINTNER	It flows across the ground. Look, look!
BRIDE	(*terrified*) I see animals of fire running through the corn.
WOMAN	No, the animals are not burning, but between them something burns.
BRIDE	Look, look – what is that great dark figure standing above them?
WOMAN	I see the light on his face.
BRIDE	It is him!
WOMAN	It's him! It's him!
BRIDE	(*screams*) It is Samson! I see his hair angry in the flame-light. I am afraid, father. (*The* 1ST SUITOR *enters with his companions. The red light now burns fiercely.*)
VINTNER	What has the man done?
1ST SUITOR	**Three hundred foxes he has caught and took firebrands and turned tail to tail and put a firebrand in the midst between two tails. And when he had set the brands on fire, he let them go into our standing corn and burnt up both the shocks and also the corn with the vineyards and olives.**
VINTNER	(*appalled*) This has he done?
3RD SUITOR	Ay, this he has done because you took his wife and gave her to our companion.
VINTNER	(*to* 1ST SUITOR) You are my kin now. Speak for us. What say you, son-in-law?

1ST SUITOR	I say burn them who have brought the fire to our people.
VINTNER	(*eagerly*) Ay, the Jews, the Jews. Burn them!
1ST SUITOR	And I say burn the friends of the Jews.
VINTNER	(*eagerly*) Ay, burn them. They are as bad and worse. Burn them!
1ST SUITOR	Let all Philistines remember the fire that Samson hath kindled.
VINTNER	(*savagely*) We shall remember!
1ST SUITOR	Let the vengeance of Dagon consume the enemies of our people.
VINTNER	Ay – let them be all consumed.
1ST SUITOR	And let the friends of our enemies burn with them.
VINTNER	Ay, let it be so! (*The* 1ST SUITOR *indicates to his companions that they should set fire to the* VINTNER'S *property. They start to do so. There are screams of terror from the women. The* VINTNER *throws himself upon the* 1ST SUITOR.)
VINTNER	What are you doing? Are you as mad as he?
1ST SUITOR	Only by a madness as great as his shall his madness be defeated. (*shouts*) Fire the vineyards! Fire the houses! Let not one child of this accursed clan escape!

SCENE 11 SAMSON'S CAMP AT ROCK ELAM

A cave in the mountain which SAMSON has made his headquarters. MANOAH argues with him.

MANOAH (*wearily*) Samson, Samson, this one-man war against a whole people is ridiculous. In the end you cannot win.

SAMSON In the end our people will follow me and we shall win. I suppose.

MANOAH You're not even sure?

SAMSON The voice says what it has always said. I am to begin to free the people. Begin.

MANOAH Alright – say we win. What will we win? A devastated land, the crops all burned, the cattle dead, the sheep crying skeletons, the old men gibbering and every woman, Philistine or Jewish over the age of ten, raped by somebody or other. If it's racial purity you're working for, this also you won't get by war.

SAMSON Father – I am not making war at the moment. I am not even planning it. All I am doing is hiding up here from the Philistines.

MANOAH Of course. That's all you are doing. Except that if, by any chance, a few dozen Philistines are stupid enough to find you, you wipe them out.

SAMSON That's purely self-defence. After the burning of the Timnite and his family, I stated categorically that I would smite the Philistines, 'hip and thigh with a great slaughter', and that is a direct quote, whatever the enemy propagandists may say to the contrary – 'And after that I will cease.' That is what I said. And that is what I meant. Any conflict between us since that time has not been of my seeking.

MANOAH After they burnt the Timnite you should have

	considered the whole business fairly settled and left it alone.
SAMSON	How could I see my father-in-law and wife murdered like that and not make some nominal protest?
MANOAH	You slaughtered all the Suitors, all their retainers and three platoons of crack police cavalry. Really, Samson – for a small country your ideas of slaughter are too big. Couldn't you have just made it the Suitors?
SAMSON	Look, father, I have already stated publicly that I consider the whole unfortunate incident closed. (MANOAH *sighs deeply*.)
MANOAH	I have to tell you, my boy, that our Philistine neighbours don't feel the same way.
SAMSON	Rest for a while – take something to drink – it's a long hard climb up here.
MANOAH	Samson, I cannot rest – I cannot drink – I didn't only come to you as your father. I bring with me other reverend elders of our tribe and of the tribe of Judah. (THREE ELDERS *enter, white bearded, wearing fringes.* SAMSON *stands up, suddenly excited*.)
SAMSON	Judah has rallied to me at last! Now shall I begin!
MANOAH	They have rallied alright.
SAMSON	With the forces of Judah and our own tribe the Philistines will be certainly defeated. (*He turns to the* ELDERS.) I thank you, Elders of Judah, for your support. Send your judges to me. Let us hold council together.
1ST ELDER	Three thousand men of Judah are rallied in the valley below, Samson.
SAMSON	Judah is a lion.
2ND ELDER	And beyond them are pitched the Philistines who have spread themselves in Lehi.
SAMSON	Then, father, go quickly back to our people and have them travel speedily through the night and meet up with the power of Judah.
MANOAH	Not so quickly, Samson. Listen, listen.

3RD ELDER	Samson, knowest thou not that the Philistines are rulers over us?
SAMSON	Now shall their rule be broken, Reverend Elder.
2ND ELDER	They are rulers over us, Samson. What is this that thou hast done unto them?
SAMSON	(*puzzled*) What is this you ask now? I challenged them – they cheated me – I revenged myself – they took vengeance upon the innocent – again and finally I answered them with great slaughter – and after that the matter should have rested so.
1ST ELDER	And now their great army is pitched in Judah and spread in Lehi.
SAMSON	But the men of Judah are three thousand and fearless.
1ST ELDER	The men of Judah honour their treaty with the Philistines.
SAMSON	(*astounded*) Why then do you come to me?
2ND ELDER	(*embarrassed*) This is what we ask the Philistines. 'Why are ye come up against us?' we ask.
3RD ELDER	And they answer 'To bind up Samson are we come up. To do to him as he hath done to us.'
2ND ELDER	So we are come to bind thee that we may deliver thee into the hand of the Philistines. (SAMSON *is dumbstruck by their submissiveness*.)
SAMSON	(*to* MANOAH *quietly*) And you father, do you also come to deliver me to the enemy?
MANOAH	I come to you as a father, not as an Elder of our tribe.
SAMSON	And as a father, what do you tell me, father?
MANOAH	As a father I tell you to escape – escape and fight. (*The* ELDERS *express their shock in murmurs*.)
SAMSON	And as an Elder of our tribe how do you speak?
MANOAH	(*sighs*) I say, weigh Samson in one scale and the people of Dan and Judah in the other and tell me which lies heaviest upon my heart. (SAMSON *makes up his mind and stands up*.)
SAMSON	(*to* ELDERS) **Swear unto me that our people will not fall upon**

	me themselves, for I cannot defend myself against our people.
1ST ELDER	We will bind thee fast and deliver thee into their hand; but surely we will not kill thee.
	(*He nods to the* 2ND ELDER *who produces two new cords from around his shoulder and comes forward.*)
SAMSON	You, father, shall bind me.
MANOAH	I?
SAMSON	(*gently*) You alone, father. You bind me, father.
	(MANOAH *binds him expertly and silently. The others lead* SAMSON *off.* MANOAH *looks after him expressionlessly for a moment and then walks into the next scene.*)

SCENE 12   MANOAH'S HOUSE

The MOTHER stands looking enquiringly towards MANOAH who walks into the area.

MOTHER	So where is Samson?
MANOAH	With two new cords we bound him and brought him up from the rock.
MOTHER	(*disgustedly*) There are no men left in the world but him. And then?
MANOAH	And when he came unto Lehi the Philistines shouted against him.
MOTHER	Now he was bound, they could shout.
MANOAH	Will you tell the story or shall I?
MOTHER	Tell, tell.
MANOAH	And the spirit of the Lord came mightily upon him.
MOTHER	(*triumphantly*) Of course.
MANOAH	And his bonds loosed from off his hands.
MOTHER	(*eagerly*) And then, and then?
MANOAH	And he found a new jawbone of an ass and put forth his hand and took it.
MOTHER	(*ecstatically*) My boy – my hero – my Samson. (*Lighting up at back of them to reveal* SAMSON *standing, his clothes torn, his body streaked with blood, the blood-streaked jawbone hanging from his hand. We dim the lighting on* MANOAH *and* SAMSON'S MOTHER *in the foreground to hold them frozen.* SAMSON *looks with dull horror at the jawbone in his hand.*)
SAMSON	**With the jawbone of an ass, dead upon dead.** (*Lighting comes up in the dark area around* SAMSON *to reveal group after group of Philistine dead. The lighting continues to come up until the entire area is revealed full of corpses in grotesque positions – a mute inferno of the slain.*)

	With the jaw of an ass have I slain a thousand men.
	(Disgustedly he tosses the bone away. Lighting up on MOTHER *and* MANOAH.*)*
MOTHER	And then, and then?
MANOAH	And then the men of Dan called him their judge and their captain. For this ass's bone has finally cloven our people away from the Philistines and from this time on there will be war. *(The* MOTHER *is seeing it all with ecstatic eyes.)*
MOTHER	That's my son. I always knew he would win that election. Samson – my son, the judge. *(Lights fade slowly and . . .)*

END ACT ONE

ACT TWO

SCENE 1 SAMSON'S CAMP AT ROCK ELAM

SAMSON has been a Judge of Israel for twenty years.
Now in his early forties, immensely powerful, but coarsened by the long years of guerilla warfare, he sits, moody and depressed, listening to a seemingly endless harangue from an old RABBI who is accompanied by an ELDER and his father, MANOAH.

RABBI — To put it in a nutshell, Samson, the people are tired of war, and who can blame them? A war that drags on year after year for nearly twenty years is no longer just a war, Samson. It's a way of life. And it's a life for a dog. Every Spring the crops are planted, every Summer the crops are burned. The standard of living throughout the tribes has never been lower. The young men are all fighting with you in the hills, interested only in the bloody business of warriors, our birthrate has dropped to an all time low, and the Philistines, who used to be such a nice, relaxed, civilized people, have become a rabble of blood-thirsty lunatics. Who can win such a war?

SAMSON — Wars are for fighting, Rabbi. Victory is an illusion resulting from a single successful battle. The war always continues.

RABBI — But to what end?

SAMSON — You, a rabbi, ask me about ends? I am an instrument of means, rabbi. You are the expert on ends. Tell me the end.

RABBI — I do not know the end of the Lord.

SAMSON — To the Lord there is no end. But I tell you this, Elders of the Tribes, in the war men find themselves, and each other. They stand up, are counted, recognize their friends, confront their enemies and are identified.

ELDER — And dead!

F 71

SAMSON	Dead perhaps, but identifiable. Dead as themselves.
MANOAH	(*gently*) It's an answer, Samson. But is it a good enough answer? Our shepherds use their shears for cutting throats. Our ploughmen make billhooks from their plough-shares. Our farmers-boys leave the fields.
SAMSON	To defend them.
MANOAH	To fight the Philistines. This doesn't defend fields. This burns them.
SAMSON	Father, gentlemen, I suggest you return to your villages before curfew. Afterwards I cannot be responsible for your safety.
RABBI	At least hear our case.
SAMSON	Tell it in Gaza – tell it in Ashkelon – tell it to the Philistines. Are they not in arms against me?
RABBI	Philistine threats you don't have to take so seriously. You know how they blow hard. Show a little friendship, Samson, and even after twenty years of slaughter, maybe they will respond.
SAMSON	They are committed on the heads of their gods to eliminate us. To show friendship to your enemy is idiotic.
ELDER	(*he sighs*) Aah! When we lived quietly among the gentiles, we had peace. From time to time the wilder currents of their life swept us up. But in ourselves we had peace because we knew that it was not our business. We were the victims of their history. Our own went on quietly, secretly.
RABBI	Spiritually he means. We were a subject people dispersed among the Gentiles, but spiritually we were one.
ELDER	We were born quietly.
RABBI	We lived quietly.
ELDER	We died with not much noise. Nothing to draw attention. Nothing to invite scorn, or envy, or fear of strangers.
RABBI	That was our spiritual unity, untouchable, beautiful and dedicated to the Lord.
ELDER	True we had transgressors. I hate to think of the

	mixed marriages. And the consumption of unclean foods increased all the time. I know. It was my job to check the butcher's shops.
MANOAH	There was even a certain amount of harmless idolatory. But basically the spirit of the people was sound.
RABBI	In fact, the spirit was sounder because we had these tests to contend with. Because we were peacefully surrounded by the Gentiles so we had the more to concentrate upon those small differences which preserve our peaceful identity.
SAMSON	And now you are Jews.
RABBI	We were Jews then – always.
SAMSON	Ay – Philistine Jews. Philistine citizens of the Jewish persuasion.
RABBI	That's so bad?
MANOAH	It's not so unreasonable. The people think of the old times and of the old ways and they long to return to them, even if it means a little bit of slavery here and there. After all, everything has its price.
SAMSON	And the cost of war to the enemy must be death. So we kill them, without hatred, without pleasure, without revenge.
MANOAH	What is there left to kill them with?
SAMSON	Reason – we kill them with sufficient reason. (*The* RABBI *sighs deeply*.)
RABBI	So for Samson there is reason in all this – sufficient reason.
ELDER	You're mad, Samson.
RABBI	Come, friends, there is no more to say.
ELDER	And soon for Samson's sake, no breath to say no more.
RABBI	Ay – we shall die, we shall die.
SAMSON	Yes, old man, and my young men too. And I also, most horribly will die.
RABBI	And in this end you see sufficient reason for the laying waste of the peace and quiet of us and our enemies. What is it by you, Samson? Is it glory? Is that what it is?

SAMSON	Does a meat-axe glory in cleaving meat? Does the jawbone of an ass glory in becoming a blunt instrument?
ELDER	(*indignantly*) Come on – away. He has already told us what is by him. Identity he wants for us. So with identity let us return to our graves.
RABBI	(*to* SAMSON) Alright then. Go on in your own way. Who can stop you? But at least, Samson, do us one favour. Stop visiting the woman of Sorek. A mad warrior if we have to, the Jews can take. But Delilah – it's not a nice thing, Samson, to know that one is being committed to death by a hero who, even after twenty years, cannot keep his hands off any Gentile woman dangerous enough to amuse him. Shall we go to our graves making excuses for Samson? (*He and the* ELDER *exit*.)
SAMSON	(*to* MANOAH) And you, father, no last word of advice from you?
MANOAH	What did I ever have to say to you, my boy? Do what you have to do. Who can do anything else?
SAMSON	I will. I do.
MANOAH	And Samson.
SAMSON	(*wearily*) Yes?
MANOAH	Your mother and I loved it the night they caught you not with this Delilah but with the Harlot before, the one from Gaza. And you carried from Gaza the stone gates to the top of Mount Hebron. We loved it. Everybody loved it! You know, even when they criticize you and shake their heads and make such a performance over how terrible it all is, what you are doing – our people admire you.
SAMSON	I am grateful for their admiration. I would be more grateful for their active support.
MANOAH	Support is different. Support may get them into even more trouble. But in their hearts, Samson, they support you.
SAMSON	(*wryly*) I'll bear it in mind the next time a Philistine spear comes in my direction.

MANOAH	(*pleading*) They are Jews, Samson. I know it is difficult sometimes, but it's a duty on us to love all Jews. Try, eh? Soon I'll come to see you again. I'll bring you some of Mother's honey cakes. Alright? And please – try. I must say – you're becoming gentler with the years, my son. You never shouted at them once.
SAMSON	(*wearily*) I'm gentle with fatigue. Go in peace, father.
MANOAH	That's right. Peace to everyone – even the Philistine Jews, eh son?
SAMSON	Peace, peace.
MANOAH	You don't mind my saying so, son, but keep away a little bit from that Sorek woman. Take it easy, eh? It's bring prophesied here and there by a few of the Prophets that she could be your downfall. For my part it's nothing, but your mother keeps on the whole time. She completely disapproves.
SAMSON	I too – totally.
MANOAH	So – take it easy, eh? (*He exits.*)

SCENE 2 DELILAH'S HOUSE AT SOREK

DELILAH is braiding her hair in front of a large bronze mirror held by a MAID.

MAID	So handsome he was, so angry and wild. It's funny how exciting a man's anger can be.
DELILAH	You gave him my answer as I instructed?
MAID	Exactly. I said, 'My Mistress says that she waits for her Lord, she longs for her master, she languishes for her lover.'
DELILAH	You fool. I never said that.
MAID	(*puzzled*) But Madam, you did.
DELILAH	I never did. I said 'I wait for my Lord.'
MAID	So you did. And then afterwards you sighed and spoke the rest.
DELILAH	But you stupid, stupid girl. The rest I said for myself – not for him.
MAID	(*smiles*) Oh but Madam, it's a great encouragement to men to hear such things. It makes lions of them. And, oh that angry young Captain who brought the message, like a mountain lion he came down to the valley.
DELILAH	Will you please stop exciting yourself over a bad-tempered little bandit and fix this damned hair for me.
MAID	(*put out*) Yes, Madam. (*She fiddles with* DELILAH'S *hair, adding to her irritation.*)
DELILAH	What is he anyway but a rough, crude, mountain bandit, middle-aged and over-weight?
MAID	(*thoughtfully*) I think just a little time with me and he would become quite courtly. These very strong men are often strong simply for fear of being weak, aren't they, my lady?
DELILAH	(*impatiently*) I'm not talking about your little Captain, fool.
MAID	(*sighs*) He's not mine, Madam. I'm just dreaming.

DELILAH	Well then, if he's not yours yet after so much dreaming, I really doubt your prowess as a woman. These mountain goats seduce very easily.
MAID	Well, of course, all that fighting and waiting in caves does make them rather eager.
DELILAH	Well then, why do you take so long to bring your little bull to stud?
MAID	He's a funny boy. Keeps telling me I'm unclean. And he, beautiful as he is, stinks like a camel. The life they lead is very unhygenic. There, Madam. Oh that looks beautiful. (DELILAH *studies her hair in the bronze mirror which the* MAID *holds up for her and makes a few minor adjustments.*)
DELILAH	That will do. Leave me now. (*The* MAID *bows and exits.* DELILAH *picks up the mirror and studies herself again.*) I wait for my Lord. I long for my master, I languish for my lover. (*She puts the mirror down and continues speaking to the audience.*) Why do we say such things? To try and make them true? It's a kind of magic, a sort of praying, a premium on our hopelessness. The truth is that I am the occasional instrument of pleasure of a wild man out of the hills who neither pays me nor protects me, nor offers me even the distant hope of a regular contract. And the fact is that in his absence I am disturbed not because he isn't here, but because he is somewhere else. It isn't his non-existence in my life which ruins everything, but his existence. If only he didn't exist, how then would I long for him and languish for him, but never waste my life waiting for him again. What an unprofitable profession it is to be a mistress. And intensely irksome in a case like this where the wretched man has not even a wife to excuse him. I simply cannot understand what I am doing in such an absurd situation, and yet, is there a woman anywhere who, by her fear of unhappiness, doesn't make even the happiest situations absurdly miserable? How often do we

	say, 'I only want to be happy' – as if it were a small enough thing to ask of a destiny which, as a general rule, keeps the millions of our insatiable species in a state of chronic unhappiness. But, my god, it's true – I only want to be happy! (*The* MAID *enters.*)
DELILAH	He's here so soon?
MAID	No, Madam. It's another gentleman. He's very pressing. Not bad-looking.
DELILAH	Tell him I am engaged. (*At which point the* PHILISTINE NOBLE, *previously called the* FIRST SUITOR, *enters.*)
NOBLE	A woman is never so unengaged as when she waits for her lover. (DELILAH *indicates to the* MAID *that she should exit, which she does.*)
DELILAH	Since you are so well informed, Sir, you will also know that it is unsafe for you to be here and will, therefore, excuse my lack of hospitality and leave.
NOBLE	We observe his movements as closely as you do, and there is time. Do you not feel that your entertainment of Samson is a betrayal of our people?
DELILAH	We do not discuss military tactics in bed.
NOBLE	Well, that's a pity then for it's an excellent battleground. (*He studies a tablet in his hand.*) In the past month he has visited you three times. It's a sharp decline of appetite, Madam. After all, do a man's needs vary so sharply? (DELILAH, *who has her own doubts anyway, now wants only to get definite information.*)
DELILAH	At least take some wine before you go.
NOBLE	Another time when you don't wait so anxiously upon the coming of an occasional friend.
DELILAH	Who is she?
NOBLE	She?
DELILAH	What is it with Samson? Tell me, tell me.
NOBLE	Why should I disturb the serene pool of your contented life?
DELILAH	To hell with your heavy poetics, who is the bitch?

NOBLE	*(calmly)* We have no information.
DELILAH	*(defensively)* Learn this then – our love is unique.
NOBLE	Come now. Supposing I concede that you are more woman than the run of women, and he more man –
DELILAH	That he certainly is, so leave before your broken neck proves it. (*The* NOBLE *continues unconcernedly.*)
NOBLE	In which case the battle between you will be more than ordinary.
DELILAH	Look Sir, if you must have a report for your fellows in Gaza, then tell them that my understanding with the man is perfect, that I am utterly content, deliriously happy and I hope it pleases them. But if it doesn't, let them come here in force, wait with me for my Lord, attend my pleasure with him, and die most violently.
NOBLE	Well spoken. You are a Samsonian patriot. Nevertheless, one who couples with an enemy is not necessarily any enemy.
DELILAH	Once these superfine Philistine discussions amused me. They always led to undistinguished love-making – but the talk was titillating. (*she sighs*) I've lost the taste for it.
NOBLE	With what eager regret do women become slaves.
DELILAH	*(defensively)* No woman has more ambition than to be the slave of such a man.
NOBLE	Well, then perhaps, since you are so satisfied with it, I will leave you in your slavish insecurity and return when Samson has another slave and you no master. (*He starts to exit.*)
DELILAH	Samson has another? (*The* NOBLE *doesn't reply, but he hesitates for a moment.* DELILAH *confronts him.*) Do you say he has another?
NOBLE	Our information says that he no longer visits you nightly.
DELILAH	But the campaign has been intense of late.
NOBLE	Indeed the war continues. But formerly he was killing daily, and yet still keeping long and regular nights.

DELILAH	Then why do you plague me, why?
NOBLE	Because the information we have indicates quite clearly (and your aching body cannot deny it, Madam) that the man is growing tired of you.
DELILAH	(*scornfully*) He tired? He's tired when he leaves me and at no other time.
NOBLE	Then let us agree that it is taking him longer to recuperate after each visit.
DELILAH	I shall point you out to him, my friend, and watch him smash you like a large blue fly.
NOBLE	The loyalty of one so certain to be betrayed is most touching. Goodnight, Madam. I wish you a sweet, if final encounter with your lion.
DELILAH	You know something. What is it you know?
NOBLE	Simply that sooner or later he must betray you.
DELILAH	How do you know it?
NOBLE	From a common experience of the war between our species.
DELILAH	Philistines and Jews are not different species.
NOBLE	But Man and Woman are. Sooner or later he will betray you. Another woman is the least of causes. He has religious mission, professional vocation, historic commitment, crude land hunger and the pressures of all that he has been and done to drive him forward and away from you. It is more than a regiment of Delilahs. (DELILAH *is finally overcome and unable to argue.*)
DELILAH	Oh gods yes, it must be so. I know it, I know it.
NOBLE	Then use the only defence a woman has against such male power.
DELILAH	What can I do? I love him.
NOBLE	(*triumphantly*) At last, the simple, bitter cry of vulnerable womanhood – the cry that shatters the world around desperate lovers.
DELILAH	I cannot help it.
NOBLE	The rest of the world-shattering cry.
DELILAH	What shall I do?
NOBLE	Betray him first, and totally. Love is a licence for treachery.

DELILAH   Never. (*a pause*) What is it you ask me to do?
NOBLE   **Entice him and see wherein his great strength lieth, and by what means we may prevail against him that we may bind him to afflict him.**
DELILAH   Oh no, no. Why should I do it?
NOBLE   Because you love him and because you will lose him and because we will give thee, every one of us, eleven hundred pieces of silver. It is not the same as a great love, but, properly invested, it is more permanent. (DELILAH *is dumbstruck by the awfulness of her interest in the propositions.*) Do you hear me, lady?
DELILAH   I hear you, serpent. Go glide in the dust forever. (*The* NOBLE *smiles, bows slightly, and exits.* DELILAH *looking at him the while with utter contempt. After he exits her expression changes; she whispers ecstatically*) I wait for my Lord, I long for my master, I languish for my lover. (*with furious venom*) The lying, treacherous, hateful, randy dog! (*Her mood changes again. She appears to be calculating.*) Eleven hundred pieces of silver each from one thousand Philistine nobles – why, that's nearly a million. More than a million. About a million. (*desperately*) Gods, if only I could be certain he would love me forever, I would not sell him for the world. But what man's love lasts forever? And a thousand times eleven hundred – yes, it is more than a million. (*She calculates thoughtfully as she turns to fix her hair, studying herself in the bronze mirror. She is very thoughtful.*)

SCENE 3 OUTSIDE DELILAH'S HOUSE

The MAID sits on her haunches, waiting. She starts and gets to her feet as SAMSON, accompanied by DAN, a young captain, enters.

MAID   Who is it? (DAN *has his drawn sword in his hand.*)
DAN   It is the man from the hills. (*The* MAID *bows.*)
MAID   My Mistress waits for her lord.
SAMSON   Thank you. (*to* DAN) Don't hang around all night, my boy. There's no danger here.
DAN   (*stubbornly*) I will keep guard. (SAMSON *smiles, shrugs, nods to the* MAID *and enters* DELILAH'S *house.* DAN *stands stiffly on guard. The* MAID *looks him up and down admiringly.*)
MAID   Will you spend the whole night here, Captain, I mean just standing there with that terrifying sword?
DAN   I will do my duty, woman.
MAID   Oh yes, I know. You always do, and I really admire you for it. But it gets very cold here at nights in this season. I'll bring you a little wine to warm you.
DAN   You don't seem ever to understand, woman. I am a Nazarite like my lord. We don't drink wine.
MAID   Of course. How stupid of me. (*she laughs*) It just seems so funny that people should have moral principles about keeping warm at night.
DAN   (*impatiently*) That's not the point. Oh I can't explain.
MAID   Well, I would never understand anyway. Is it alright for you to keep warm in my tent?
DAN   (*surlily*) Thank you, but it won't be necessary. (*The* MAID *now approaches* DAN *and standing close to him looks up into his face charmingly. He looks away from her, staring towards his duty.*)
MAID   I know that Nazarites are allowed to go with women.

DAN (*angrily*) Of course we are.
MAID (*laughs*) Perhaps you would like me to find you a woman for the night. (*she laughs again*) It is an excellent way of keeping warm.
DAN (*roughly*) It is not necessary – but I thank you.
MAID Oh, please don't bother. It's only common hospitality. I mean, I know that we are unclean and all that but I could find you a woman and make her bathe. Would that be alright?
DAN I tried to explain to you last time. Unclean doesn't mean that you need a bath.
MAID Oh yes, I do remember. I am so stupid. Would *you* like a bath? I know you don't get many opportunities up there in those wild hills.
DAN (*doubtfully*) Well – a bath would be pleasant.
MAID (*eagerly*) Oh, wonderful. I'll prepare it for you myself. I prepare the most beautiful baths. My Mistress is mad about them. And I scrub and massage delightfully.
DAN Thank you but that won't be necessary.
MAID Oh, please don't worry about it. It's part of our law of hospitality. We just cannot allow a stranger to take a bath on his own. Now, you keep guard there and I'll make everything ready for us. Oh, it's such a beautiful night. Though, of course, it will get very, very cold. (*The* MAID *exits leaving* DAN *somewhat uncertain about what he has committed himself to.*)

SCENE 4   DELILAH'S HOUSE

SAMSON and DELILAH *lie together on a great couch of fur skins.* ...

DELILAH	Do you love me? (SAMSON *doesn't reply.*) Oh, how I love my Lord! (DELILAH *stirs irritably.*) Are you well my Lord? (SAMSON *sighs, or grunts, or both.*) Can I bring my Lord something? Something to drink? Would my Lord eat? (*She gently strokes his shoulders.*) How hard and knotted are my Lord's muscles. I shall massage your shoulders. Turn about. (SAMSON *gets up from the couch, frustrating her.*)
SAMSON	I must leave.
DELILAH	So soon?
SAMSON	I must.
DELILAH	But why so soon? What battles will you direct in the middle of the night? Stay till morning I beg of you.
SAMSON	I must away.
DELILAH	(*scornfully*) What do you know of love?
SAMSON	Delilah – not that old debate. I love you and you have comforted and restored me. My mind is clear again. I see the way I must go. And so I leave you with love in my heart.
DELILAH	So leaving is proof of loving?
SAMSON	Say no more, lady. I'll stay.
DELILAH	Should I kiss the hem of that stinking ill-cured ancient lion's skin in gratitude?
SAMSON	You ask me to stay and so I stay. What more?
DELILAH	(*furiously*) Will you not stay because you want it, and not because I ask it?
SAMSON	You'll break my mind, sweetheart, with these everlasting riddles. Come to bed. I'll stay till the hour before sunrise.
DELILAH	No.
SAMSON	No?

DELILAH	Go now.
SAMSON	You want me to go?
DELILAH	(*uncertainly*) Yes.
SAMSON	Why then I'll go.
DELILAH	Before you go –
SAMSON	Yes?
DELILAH	Answer me one simple question, simply.
SAMSON	Yes.
DELILAH	Do you love me?
SAMSON	Is this a simple question to be answered between the middle of the night and the hour before dawn?
DELILAH	(*bursts out*) It's a question that can be answered in the movement of an eye or the sighing of a breath.
SAMSON	Tonight my breath rattled like a hunted gazelle. So, it is proven I love you. Will I leave or shall we to bed again?
DELILAH	(*irritatedly*) Oh, do as you want.
SAMSON	(*too reasonably*) But I would do what you want, my honey creature – if you could make up your mind.
DELILAH	(*pleadingly*) Oh Samson, my soul would rest forever if I did but surely know you loved me. Prove, love, that you love me. (SAMSON *takes in this fundamental female request slowly and turns to the audience, who remember with him another woman earlier in the story who made the same request – and its consequences.*)
SAMSON	(*to audience*) Familiar, isn't it? From the first woman to the last, the same impossible demand echoes, an unanswerable question, the cry of a lamb to the rocks. (*He turns to* DELILAH.) Sweet lamb of Sorek, how shall I prove it? Can a man dam up the anxious disbelief of a woman who is incapable of loving herself? And if he does contain it, that irritating trickle of uncertainty, will it not in the end burst its banks and drown him? (DELILAH *doesn't reply.*)

SAMSON	(*with gentle resignation*) Alright then. Tell me, love, how shall I prove love? (*to audience*) Now it comes. It comes now.
DELILAH	**Tell me lord, I pray thee, wherein thy great strength lieth and wherewith thou mightest be bound to afflict thee.**
SAMSON	(*to audience*) For answering this question I am remembered in history as a man only. (*turns to* DELILAH) **If thou bind me with seven green withies that were never dried, then shall I be weak and be as another man.**
DELILAH	(*unbelievingly*) Seven green withies?
SAMSON	Alternatively, maybe I'm just a very powerful man. Did this explanation ever occur to you?
DELILAH	Of course. You must be extraordinary otherwise I wouldn't feel this extraordinary love for you.
SAMSON	(*hopefully*) Can we leave the question then, and go to bed?
DELILAH	Maybe. No – there must be some magic as well. After all you don't exercise regularly, your diet is short on protein, you don't drink wine, and you're too dependent on sex and violence to be a holy man. (*impatiently*) Tell me the secret, Samson. Prove you love me.
SAMSON	(*resignedly*) Seven green withies.
DELILAH	(*eagerly*) I think there are seven here somewhere. (*She goes off to look for them.*)
SAMSON	(*to audience*) I know that there are men lying in wait about the tent. They wait while my guard takes his bath and I answer Love's deadly catechism. (DELILAH *returns, she mimes a bunch of withies and mimes again her binding of* SAMSON *with them.*)
SAMSON	(*mildly to* DELILAH) Supposing there are enemies lying in wait?
DELILAH	My love protects you.
SAMSON	Supposing it fails?
DELILAH	Are you afraid to test it?

SAMSON	Anyone who cares for his love should be afraid to test her. (DELILAH *kneels to bind his legs.*)
DELILAH	Tell me if I hurt you.
SAMSON	You will, you will. (DELILAH *finishes binding his legs.*)
DELILAH	(*delightedly*) Who would have thought it? Seven green withies. (*She is suddenly alarmed.*) What sound was that?
SAMSON	(*mildly*) It's the sound of the men lying in wait.
DELILAH	(*hysterically*) **The Philistines be upon thee Samson!** (SAMSON *is miming his bound hands and legs. Now he mimes breaking the withies.*)
DELILAH	(*aghast*) **You broke the withies as a thread of tow is broken when it toucheth the fire.** (she calls) **His strength is not known!** (*The sound offstage of the men lying in wait subsides at her signal.*)
SAMSON	I believe you have something to say to me.
DELILAH	(*with suppressed, hurt fury*) **Behold thou has mocked me and told me lies. Thou loves me not.** (*She throws herself down on the couch distraught.* SAMSON *turns to the audience.*)
SAMSON	(*to audience*) There are two overwhelming questions in my story. The first is, what is God doing? We shall continue to examine this question after the present tableau reaches its inevitable conclusion. The second is, what am I doing? I know she will betray me, I lie again, but in the end I will tell her and it will be so. (*to* DELILAH) **If they bind me fast with new ropes that were never occupied, then shall I be weak and be as other men.**
DELILAH	(*eagerly*) I'll bring new ropes.
SAMSON	(*to audience*) Later the lies become a little wild. (*to* DELILAH) **If thou weavest the seven locks of my head with**

	the web, then shall I be weak and be as other men.
	(DELILAH *turns on him furiously*.)
DELILAH	I'm sick of it.
	How canst thou say 'I love thee' when thy heart is not with me? Thou hast mocked me these three times and hast not told me wherein thy great strength lieth.
	How canst thou say 'I love thee' when thy heart is not with me? How canst thou say 'I love thee'? How canst thou say 'I love'? How canst thou say? How canst thou? How canst? How?
	(DELILAH *continues to mime the questions endlessly*.)
SAMSON	(*wearily*)
	She presses daily with her words so that my soul is vexed unto death.
DELILAH	How canst thou say 'I love thee'? How canst thou say 'I love'? How canst thou say? How canst thou?
SAMSON	Enough! My soul is vexed unto death.
DELILAH	How canst thou say 'I love thee'? How canst thou say? How canst thou? How?
SAMSON	Enough! Enough!
DELILAH	How canst? (SAMSON *seizes her and puts his hand over her mouth*.)
SAMSON	So here is my heart, woman. Eat it.
	There hath not come a razor upon my head for I have been a Nazarite unto God from my mother's womb. If I be shaven then my strength will go from me and I shall become weak and like any other man.
DELILAH	Is that all?
SAMSON	That's all.
DELILAH	(*sullenly*) I don't believe it.
SAMSON	It's true.
DELILAH	You're making a fool of me again.
SAMSON	That's my secret.
DELILAH	You don't love me. You never loved me. I shall go away.

SAMSON (*wearily*) Go – stay. Believe or not. My soul is vexed unto death.
DELILAH Not too tired to come to bed, I expect.
SAMSON Go to. I will follow.
DELILAH (*triumphantly*) Tonight we shall lie with a razor between us.
SAMSON Go to. Let me think awhile on what we are about. (DELILAH *exits*.)
SAMSON (*to audience*) I am a tired lion with a compulsion to eat honey. I see it there golden, luminous and infinitely satisfying. And I must eat to satiate my ravenous leonine soul which afterwards will purr and sleep for a little, till waking it roars in agony of need for honey once again. In less poetic terms I am addicted to her and deprived must sustain acutely painful symptoms of withdrawal; an idiotic male syndrome. But I have an excuse. As God's instrument I can attribute all that happens to me to His obscure intentions. Has God a God to provide Him with such an excuse? (*He yawns profoundly.*) Exhausting, isn't it? (*He sighs and rests on the couch and falls asleep.* DELILAH *re-enters. She studies him for a moment.*)
DELILAH All men look pitiful asleep, pale, troubled, breathing hard and stupid. As an act of belief I tell myself that this heavy sleeper is a mythical lover for whom I forsook my people and my gods. I prayed to him as he bore down on me. Satisfy me. Fill me. Shoot me full of your honey, for I am empty again. Fill me, great roaring heart, fill the cold and empty moon below my breasts with hot honey of the sun, my lion. Bear down on me, my beast – (*A Philistine* BARBER *enters tentatively as she speaks.*)
DELILAH What the hell do you want?
BARBER You called for a barber, lady.
DELILAH Was that what it was, my remembered ecstasy – a call for a barber?
BARBER I thought I heard a call, lady. Though his lord-

	ship there is not exactly prone to my art. He is a hairy gentleman, isn't he, my lady? Beautiful head of hair. Too good for a gentleman really. Looks to me as if he'll keep it right into his old age. The follicles have a strong appearance. People don't realize how diet affects the hair. (DELILAH *seems dazed as the* BARBER *chatters on.*)
DELILAH	You have a razor?
BARBER	Of course, my lady. As my old father used to say, one of the best known barbers in Gaza he was, 'Whether you be barber, soldier or just a fool, never travel without your tool.' He was a bit coarse the old fellow but a first-class barber, may he rest in peace. I wish I was half as good.
DELILAH	Give me the razor.
BARBER	Give it to you, my lady?
DELILAH	Give it to me. (*The* BARBER *produces his razor from his bag.*)
BARBER	This is my beard razor. For the hair you don't need it so sharp. Which was his lordship thinking of having trimmed? (DELILAH *deeply absorbed and very tensely, with adoration and ambivalence, holds the razor in one hand and gently draws up the long locks of* SAMSON'S *hair with the other.*)
DELILAH	Are these the strings that bind me to a man? (*The* BARBER *is watching her curiously.*)
BARBER	It could well be, lady. A lot of ladies are much affected by a gentleman's fine hair.
DELILAH	(*without looking at him*) Get out.
BARBER	What do you say, lady? (DELILAH *looks at him with coldly murderous venom. The* BARBER *backs away frightened but persistent.*) You surely won't do the job yourself, my lady? It's a small trade but skilled withal. A bad haircut can mar a gentleman's appearance and ruin his chances for life. It's a dangerous weapon in the wrong hands, lady.
DELILAH	(*quietly*) Then it will cut a fool's throat. (*The* BARBER *sees that she means it and backs away hurriedly.*)

BARBER	Do it, lady, if the fancy has taken you. I'll not say a word. I'm a good union man but I'll not say a word. (*He backs offstage.* DELILAH *looks back at* SAMSON. *Her eyes look slowly across his body from his feet to his head. She gently takes the seven locks of his hair in her hand. She kneels and touches them with her cheek and her lips.*)
DELILAH	Ah love! (*with deep feeling*) Love! (*Then holding the seven locks in one hand she cuts them one by one.*) Love! Love! Love! Love! Love! Love! (*Then as she looks at the seven locks in her hand horror strikes her, her hand opens and she drops them to the floor. Then the razor drops.*)
DELILAH	(*with deep grief*) Ah love. (SAMSON *wakes suddenly from his sleep.*)
SAMSON	(*alarmed*) The Philistines are upon me! (*He sees her and his frightened expression fades and he smiles.*) Ah Delilah!
DELILAH	**The Philistines are upon thee, Samson!**
SAMSON	(*still smiling*) Not again. You would not play so bad a joke again.
DELILAH	(*with mounting hysteria*) It wasn't true, was it? You lied to me, didn't you, didn't you lie to me? Say you did. Please tell me it was a lie.
SAMSON	(*puzzled*) What?
DELILAH	The hair. The hair. (*She looks down at his locks on the floor. He follows her gaze. His face drains of blood. He looks back at her slowly and she knows now, finally, both that he loves her and that he is lost. As they look at one another with the growing terror of lovers whose loss is irrecoverable, the lords of the Philistines, heavily armed, silently enter barring* SAMSON'S *retreat.*)

END ACT TWO

ACT THREE

SCENE 1   MANOAH'S HOUSE

MANOAH dictates to the SCRIBE who writes laboriously on a parchment.

MANOAH	Read it back.
SCRIBE	And she said, 'The Philistines be upon thee, Samson.'
MANOAH	Yes. That's right 'And he woke out of his sleep.'
SCRIBE	(*writing*) 'And he woke'... Do you have to say 'Out of his sleep?' If he woke it's clear he was asleep.
MANOAH	To me it sounds better to say 'And he woke out of his sleep.'
SCRIBE	I'm just making a suggestion that's all.
MANOAH	I'm grateful for your suggestions, but please take it down my way. So – 'He woke out of his sleep.' (*The* SCRIBE *shrugs and writes as* SAMSON'S MOTHER *enters. She seems much older, broken and perhaps a little unhinged. She wears mourning. Her tone is bitter and querulous.*)
MOTHER	(*argumentively*) His hair cut so a girl with no breasts could lead him to the place of execution.
MANOAH	(*patiently*) We are working, my dear.
MOTHER	I taught him this.
MANOAH	Yes. True. But now we are working.
MOTHER	Oh, my boy Samson, what a judge you were, except for those women.
SCRIBE	(*aside to* MANOAH) Maybe I should take the opportunity to cut some fresh pens. Once she starts –
MANOAH	Good idea. (*The* SCRIBE *exits.*)
MOTHER	And now where is he? Lying in the filth with the fleas nesting in his hair stubble!
MANOAH	Make some cheese. Bake. Do something. It will take your mind off. (SAMSON'S MOTHER, *totally involved in her emotions, ignores him.*)

MOTHER	Those filthy, uncircumcized pigs with that secret weapon of theirs, that rotten lousy Dagonish priestess, that sacred prostitute, that Delilah! (*She spits out three times.*)
MANOAH	Easy, easy, mother.
MOTHER	Easy? Easy! When everything is broken in little pieces around him? When the whole world comes down on him, there is left only his mother. Should she be easy?
MANOAH	We've been over it before. So often. For a whole year nothing else. (*She suddenly seems calm and with a slightly insane comprehension.*)
MOTHER	You know what it is?
MANOAH	What is it?
MOTHER	This whole life of his is a sermon.
MANOAH	So, good. Leave me to write it and perhaps by the time I've finished I'll see the message and so it'll be a proper sermon. Alright?
MOTHER	Oh no! This is not the end, with him rotting quietly in a dungeon with a mouse for company and the fleas biting. This is no end for a son of mine, for a hero – one whose birth was prophesied, who was raised in purity, who never had a knife touch his hair until that dirty whore got him into her clutches!
MANOAH	(*wearily*) I remember, believe me, I remember.
MOTHER	The world will remember for ever. They will curse her for ever. They will call him an idiot for ever.
MANOAH	Enough, woman.
MOTHER	Never!
MANOAH	(*roars*) Do you hear me, woman? I say enough!
MOTHER	(*sullenly*) From me you'll hear nothing. What should I say now?
MANOAH	Alright then. So let's get on with it. (*He looks around for the* SCRIBE.) Oh, where has he gone?
MOTHER	I mean, did I say something when, as a boy, he came to you and said he wanted the woman from Timnath? Did I say anything then?

MANOAH	Yes. You said why can't he marry a Jewish girl. So did I. But he didn't. He couldn't. It was his destiny.
MOTHER	I said, of course, I said. He was my only son, born when I had for years given up all hope of conceiving. Naturally, I said.
MANOAH	We know, we know the whole story. Everybody knows it.
MOTHER	(*persists*) When he was a little boy with long hair and everybody was saying 'Please, it's time Samson had a haircut. It looks ridiculous! He looks like a girl.' You don't know how I felt. I did my duty. I kept my vow to the Angel. I wanted a little boy like other little boys. But no. I kept my word.
MANOAH	And he paid for it. You think it's easy to wear long hair in a short-haired society?
MOTHER	Alright. It was hard for him too. But we of Israel are not for ourselves. We are for each other and for Jahveh. Hear, oh Israel, the Lord, thy God, the Lord is One!
MANOAH	So He heard and now *he* wakes up in darkness.
MOTHER	(*stubbornly*) Jahveh is with him still.
MANOAH	(*sighs*) I'm not so sure. Jahveh hates the weak.
MOTHER	It'll be alright in the end, you'll see. After all, what did he do that was so terrible? He loved a Philistine girl, that's all. Fool, with the career he had before him, the opportunities – thrown away for 'love'.
MANOAH	At his age love is a desperate illness. For a middle-aged judge, passion is fatal.
MOTHER	(*stubbornly*) Only because the girl was a Philistine. If she was an Israelite girl his hair would be twice as long, he would be twice as strong, he would kill twice as many Philistines and Israel would be master of the world. That's because a Jewish wife is a help to her husband.
MANOAH	How can you help who you fall in love with? I mean, don't take this wrong – but that Angel of yours –

MOTHER (*immediately on the defensive*) My Angel was a proper Angel sent by Jahveh. It's in the annals of the tribe now. It's history, Manoah. Nobody argues with Jewish history. Oh, he came like a prince, like a prince he came. In a long white silk robe with his fine brown lean features and his brilliant black eyes...

MANOAH (*sighs*) She's right. Who argues with Jewish history?

MOTHER (*carried away*) And I was working in the fields, a slave, like all our people. And suddenly he stood – his back to the shimmering sunlight, a vision, a mirage. And I was tired from the heat and the work and the long years without children. But I was handsome. Of eight sisters, I was the most beautiful. And there I was, twenty-four, a middle-aged woman already, but still handsome, and he looked at me and his face shone like the sun and I was blinded. And he spoke the words of prophesy and I fainted there in the burning sunlight. (*She seems to sink a little, reliving her ecstasy.*)

MANOAH So you fainted.

MOTHER (*defensively*) In such circumstances, any woman would faint. What's so wrong?

MANOAH I don't really want to discuss it now.

MOTHER What's to discuss? A mother-to-be has a visitation from an agel. What's so unusual?

MANOAH (*warily*) Nothing, nothing.

MOTHER (*threateningly*) This isn't the first time you've said something against my angel. Are you daring to deny the prophesy? Is that what's behind all our trouble? Is that why Samson is in this absolutely tragic situation?

MANOAH Did I say something? I said nothing, nothing.

MOTHER (*bitterly*) My son, a hero of forty-two, a little bit overweight, but still a hero, captured by the Philistines, but nevertheless a hero, sold into slavery to pigs by a cheap priestess of a low-down sex-god, but still a hero in Israel. And this

	hero's father dares to have doubts about his wife's angel. A pure Jewish Angel, and *he* dares to have doubts!
MANOAH	(*firmly*) Alright. You want the truth? He never did sound too Jewish to me. He –
MOTHER	(*appalled*) What? You're saying my angel was a foreign angel? A gentile angel? You can say that to a mother in Israel? Oh, woe is me! (*She starts to cry a little bit.*)
MANOAH	(*firmly*) Now you listen to me. You wanted this discussion. So let's have it out at last. This long white silk robe, this dark skin, these piercing black eyes, this fine aquiline nose – this is how the Philistine nobility look, isn't it?
MOTHER	(*hysterically covering her ears*) I don't want to discuss it any more!
MANOAH	(*decisively*) I am not, my dear, questioning the sincerity of your faith, but maybe this angel actually was a Philistine noble. He's riding past the fields, he sees a beautiful Israelite woman bending over, he has an idea he would like to know her better...
MOTHER	(*crying*) Blasphemer! Father of a girl-chaser! How can you say such terrible things?
MANOAH	Alright then. What was the angel's name?
MOTHER	An angel has to introduce himself formally? He didn't give a name.
MANOAH	(*shrugs*) I'm a simple shepherd of the tribe of Dan. What do I know about angels?
MOTHER	(*crying*) I'm going. I'm leaving. I won't stay here to be told I'm a loose woman and my son a bastard! God forgive me for being a woman and a mother!
MANOAH	(*shrugs*) So. Go. (*The* SCRIBE *enters.*)
SCRIBE	(*to* MANOAH) She's going? (*About to leave* SAMSON'S MOTHER *turns on* MANOAH *violently.*)
MOTHER	And another thing!
SCRIBE	(*hurriedly*) I'll come back later. (*He hurries off.*)
MOTHER	This is a boy who tore lions to pieces with his bare hands. Is that normal?

MANOAH	The whole thing was never normal.
MOTHER	This is a young man who carried the stone gates of Gaza to the top of Mount Hebron. That's a long way to carry a stone gate.
MANOAH	(*impatiently*) Who's arguing about that?
MOTHER	(*triumphantly*) Alright then. You'll admit that only those favoured by Jahveh can do such things.
MANOAH	I'll admit it wasn't normal.
MOTHER	(*conclusively*) So. What's wrong with my angel?
MANOAH	Question.
MOTHER	(*grandly*) If you wish.
MANOAH	Where was he going this boy when he tore the lion to pieces?
MOTHER	You expect me to remember every little detail?
MANOAH	(*triumphantly*) He was going to make love with the woman of Timnath. That's where.
MOTHER	So, a boy's high-spirited. What's so terrible?
MANOAH	As for the gates of Gaza –
MOTHER	(*proudly*) That will be remembered for ever. What a performance!
MANOAH	But it will also be remembered that on that night he was caught sleeping with a Harlot at Gaza.
MOTHER	Treacherous bitch! She also sold him to the Philistines. But he destroyed them every last one and for a joke carried away their gate. (*she laughs*) In those days he was always full of jokes and riddles and fun.
MANOAH	(*resignedly*) You miss the point.
MOTHER	The point is, my son is a Jewish hero and nothing else matters.
MANOAH	(*almost to himself*) But when the Timnath woman betrayed him why didn't he learn? How can I explain this?
MOTHER	She was the one who told them the answer. Out of whatever it was came forth something or other. I can't remember the exact details.
MANOAH	Strength. And sweetness. Maybe that's the answer. Jahveh gave him the strength but he had to take the sweetness. For who can live by strength alone?

MOTHER   (*contemptuously*) Sweet little slut, that one from Timnath, who giggled a lot.
MANOAH   (*sighs*) She did and she burned for it. She was fifteen.
MOTHER   (*savagely*) All Philistines should die at such an age.
MANOAH   All love should die at such an age. Later on it kills you.
MOTHER   (*impatiently*) Listen! I can't stand here talking with you all day. The older you get the more you talk. Talk. Talk. Talk. I've got things to get on with.
MANOAH   I talk?
MOTHER   (*aggressively*) You want to talk or you want to eat? If you want to eat let me get on with it. I don't talk. I do. That's Jewish. (*She exists busily.* MANOAH *sighs deeply, shakes his head and turns his attention back to the writing on the table. The* SCRIBE *comes in.*)
SCRIBE   She's really gone?
MANOAH   (*impatiently*) Your writing is terrible. Read it back to me. (*The* SCRIBE *bends over the parchment and reads.*)
SCRIBE   'And he woke out of his sleep.' (*He shrugs distastefully at the phrase.*)
MANOAH   Now! 'And she said, "The Philistines be upon thee, Samson." And he woke out of his sleep and said, "I will go out as at other times before and shake myself." ' (*The* SCRIBE *stops writing and looks at* MANOAH *questioningly.*)
MANOAH   (*testily*) Why are you stopping now?
SCRIBE   'Shake myself.' I don't like 'shake myself.'
MANOAH   Put it down, put it down. You can make the refinements later. What?
SCRIBE   'I will go out as at other times before and shake myself.'
MANOAH   That's right. 'And he wist not that the Lord was departed from him.' (*The* SCRIBE *takes it down.*) 'But the Philistines took him and . . . , (*he hesitates*) . . . and . . .'

SCRIBE	(*gently*) I know. I know.
MANOAH	(*firmly*) 'And put out his eyes and brought him down to Gaza and bound him with fetters of brass and he did grind in the prison house.'
SCRIBE	(*writing*) 'And he did grind in the prison house.' (*The* SCRIBE *sighs deeply*.) So, that's how it ends.
MANOAH	No. It is not ended yet. But put it down.
SCRIBE	It's down. It's down. (*The sound of distant grinding is heard.*)

SCENE 2   THE PRISON HOUSE IN GAZA

In the prison house below the Temple of Dagon in Gaza, SAMSON sits in pillowed comfort in clean robes, unfettered, smoking a water pipe, being attended by a young GIRL in the white silk dress of a novitiate. He is relaxed, overweight, degenerate and neatly blinded, his eyes beautiful and empty after an expert surgical operation to remove the optic nerves.

SAMSON	It draws badly. Blow on the coal.
GIRL	Yes, sir. (*She blows gently on the coals beneath the pipe.*)
SAMSON	How old are you?
GIRL	Fifteen. Is the pipe drawing better now, sir? (SAMSON *draws on the pipe and stares at her sightlessly.*)
GIRL	You eat me with your blind eyes, sir.
SAMSON	Come closer. (*The* GIRL *comes closer.* SAMSON *feels for her throat.*)
GIRL	(*embarrassed*) I know you're used to much better than me, sir. I know it's a fantastic honour for me. I know I don't deserve it. But my mother is very ambitious for me, and I will try very hard, sir. (SAMSON'S *hand is feeling the* GIRL'S *face.*)
SAMSON	(*preoccupied*) Over this another and behind this another. Where is the ultimate face?
GIRL	I'm supposed to be quite pretty, sir. I mean, I don't think I am. But a lot of the pilgrims say I am. (*she sighs*) Of course men always say that when they want you. You can't really take it seriously. But I *think* I'm *quite* pretty.
SAMSON	Where is the ultimate face? (*He withdraws his hand hopelessly from her face and turns his blind eyes away.*)
GIRL	Well, I think I am it actually. That is why mother wanted it to be me. That is why she gave great

	gifts to the priests. (*proudly*) I am the thousandth woman dedicated to the god.
SAMSON	Have there been a thousand of you?
GIRL	Oh yes. And all conceived. I think you're marvellous. We all do.
SAMSON	In war and sex everyone lies.
GIRL	(*overwhelmed*) I am the thousandth bride of God's Prick. It's wonderful.
SAMSON	What did you call me?
GIRL	I'm sorry, sir. Did I say something wrong? I mean, 'Revered Phallus of Omnipotent Dagon' is a bit difficult for the ordinary people. And God's Prick is sort of homey. When I have your son, sir, I will call him after you.
SAMSON	Thank you. But can you be sure it will be a son?
GIRL	(*alarmed*) Oh, it must be. The girls are sacrificed immediately. But the boys are brought up in a special school to be warriors, supermen, through whose strength our people will be forever unconquerable. (*urgently*) Oh, please sir, will you not lay with me now? I die for you. Kill me, sir. Make me live, sir. Do it quickly. Now. Now.
SAMSON	Smoke a little first. (*He hands her the pipe. The* GIRL *draws on it greedily.*)
SAMSON	(*muses*) So I, a blunt instrument of Destiny, the secret weapon of Jahveh, have become God's Prick. (*he laughs*) There's a joke there somewhere.
GIRL	Oh – this is strong.
SAMSON	Smoke, smoke.
GIRL	Is it usual, sir?
SAMSON	Essential.
GIRL	I wish for the sake of my mother to do everything well, sir.
SAMSON	I'm sure you will.
GIRL	Thank you. (*shyly*) You knew my mother well once, sir.
SAMSON	(*yawning*) Was she – a Temple girl?
GIRL	(*indignantly*) Certainly not, sir. She was the Great Harlot of Gaza, and for her sake you did the impossible, bearing on your back the stone gates

	of the city to the crest of Mount Hebron. (*proudly*) Did ever a woman receive a greater compliment than that?
SAMSON	So you are the daughter of that great Priestess?
GIRL	(*with simple pride*) I am, sir. And one day, if I am good, I will be as great a whore as she has been. She's retired now, an old woman of nearly forty but still does good work for the god. She conducts the finishing school at our Temple and speaks often of the monument you raised to her.
SAMSON	(*his curiosity aroused*) Does she also speak of how she betrayed me to the Philistines, and how I killed very many of them?
GIRL	(*indignantly*) Certainly not, sir. My mother is a woman and prefers to remember only the nicer things. Your superb compliment to her is the poor lady's sweetest memory. She was very upset about you and Delilah. She said Delilah wasn't professional. (*impatiently*) Oh please lay with me now, sir. If you don't it will be my first black mark and I do so want to be professional.
SAMSON	Come, alien, let me help you in your eternal homework.
GIRL	(*delightedly*) Oh, thank you, sir. (*ecstatically*) You are the greatest lover of my great harlot mother. How happy she will be when I tell her I pleased you well. (*She starts to embrace him very expertly.*)
SAMSON	Oh yes. Your little teeth are cunning, little bitch-fox.
GIRL	If I please you greatly, sir, will you reward me?
SAMSON	Of course – with a son, a super-warrior.
GIRL	(*subtly*) Yes, of course. But will you also tell me some little secret?
SAMSON	You too!
GIRL	(*eagerly*) Tell me, tell me. Then I shall make you happy beyond the memory of all the others. (*She embraces him eagerly.* SAMSON *jaded as he is begins to respond when the* GIRL *withdraws.*)

GIRL	(*accusingly*) You do respond somewhat readily, sir. Is it for my particular taste or smell? Or is it quite impersonal? (*She is obvious a little hurt.*)
SAMSON	(*kindly*) No, no. It is not entirely impersonal. Go on. (*The* GIRL *continues her lovemaking and then stops again.*)
SAMSON	(*irritably*) Well, what is it, child?
GIRL	I have been calculating, sir. You have been here a year or so and for me to be the thousandth privileged one calculates a daily turnover of three such.
SAMSON	I assure you, sweet girl, few of them were as accomplished as you. Now go to it. Smoke, smoke. (*The* GIRL *smokes resentfully.*)
GIRL	(*petulantly*) Well, I think it's all a little impersonal. (*she brightens*) Unless you see me with your touch. Is it so?
SAMSON	(*edgily*) Blindness does sharpen the touch and intensify the imagination.
GIRL	(*much relieved and affected by the smoke*) Oh – I am so very happy. (*She smokes again, swoons and moans.*) Now – now – now – now. (*She faints away.* SAMSON *sighs and claps his hands. A young Philistine* PRIEST (ZOAB) *enters.*)
SAMSON	Ah, Amnon, here is another for you.
ZOAB	Amnon is off duty today. I am Zoab.
SAMSON	You are new to this post, Zoab? (ZOAB *is very refined and highly intellectual, and somewhat pompous.*)
ZOAB	I come straight from the seminary, sir.
SAMSON	(*wryly*) Good. You should be in excellent condition for the work. Take this child and service her well. I had a little trouble and much joy of her mother.
ZOAB	Yes, sir. Of course I will – but – (*He looks at the* GIRL *and hesitates.*)
SAMSON	Well, go to it, lad. There are more waiting.
ZOAB	There aren't actually, sir. This one will complete the cycle. There will be a great feast in your honour with great sacrifices to the Lord Dagon.

SAMSON	Good, good. Go to it, go.
ZOAB	Certainly, sir. May I ask a question first, sir?
SAMSON	(*sighs*) Another intellectual. Can I stop you?
ZOAB	Thank you, sir. The question of your extraordinary strength, sir, which for some twenty years was a *casus belli* between our peoples –
SAMSON	(*wearily*) Must we go into it yet again? Your woman Delilah found the secret, sold it for more than she could count and keeps (I believe) my hair as a souvenir of our short but incredibly beautiful friendship. What more is there to be said?
ZOAB	We Philistines are a rational people, sir. We find it very difficult to swallow the extraordinary myths which are the daily bread of your strange, stubborn, perverse and dangerous tribe.
SAMSON	Is it easier to believe in the strength of a fish-tailed idol of gold, saturated in dolphin oil and presiding over a continuous orgy of nymphomanic priestesses and exhausted pilgrims?
ZOAB	Oh, much easier. Our Dagon reminds us that without fertility there is nothing. Our priestesses lay with the unhappy stranger to show us that the grim wastage of life may be forgotten in the fertile transports of a joy without which living would be too dreary a process to continue. Our religion is a simple and scientific poetry. You can hardly say the same for yours.
SAMSON	I say nothing for mine. Religion and sex have never interested me very much.
ZOAB	But theology, wool and puritanism are the principal products of Israel.
SAMSON	(*irritably*) My boy, I am a middle-aged folk hero who has lost his home following. Excuse me your debate, do your job and preserve my myth.
ZOAB	(*thoughtfully*) Of course, of course. We support your myth for good reasons. After the surprise of our discovery that you were impotent –
SAMSON	(*impatiently*) It went with the hair. Some sort of traumatic shock, your doctors thought.

ZOAB (*irritatingly*) Of course, of course. No one has ever implied that you were always so –

SAMSON (*roars*) Ask Delilah!

ZOAB (*calmly*) Well, her evidence was discounted. Women lie about the potency of their men. It flatters their narcissism.

SAMSON (*stiffly*) May I remind you of the occasion on which I killed one thousand of your people with the jawbone of an ass?

ZOAB This has been carefully researched. The actual number of dead was fourteen.

SAMSON You record your figure, boy, and we will record ours. Let's see which one history remembers.

ZOAB (*undisturbed*) In any case, sir, military prowess invariably travels with erotic disinclination. The great military leaders who have not been actual pederasts have been, by and large, sexually neuter.

SAMSON (*furious*) Is it the intention of your diabolical inquisitors to drive me mad with the jejune maunderings of a seminary theoretician?

ZOAB I assure you, sir, there is nothing personal in my observations. But we do have to consider your future.

SAMSON (*wearily*) We Jews do everything that is destined for us. Always with great reluctance, but we do it.

ZOAB Come now, sir. You are almost at the end of a slightly comic career. Can you still have faith in its seriousness?

SAMSON We are always deadly serious when we make jokes.

ZOAB If I may continue. You have been a criminal against us and by your own law owe us an equal return. By the calculation of our experts this has now been made.

SAMSON (*indignantly*) But *I* have not serviced these foolish Philistine mothers.

ZOAB That is a technical detail. In symbolic principle, you have now compensated us for our losses.

SAMSON So what will you do next? Kill me a thousand

	times with the jawbone of an ass – symbolically, of course.
ZOAB	Fourteen. We might manage fourteen deaths. We are very skilful. Then of course there is castration.
SAMSON	What possible difference could that make to me?
ZOAB	But that we must reject on religious grounds. For us even the fertility of an enemy contains an element of the divine.
SAMSON	(*breathes a sight of relief*) Strange how, though they grow increasingly less decorative and useful, one would rather keep the absurd regalia of one's manhood.
ZOAB	(*thoughtfully*) Our problem now is to discover a final solution to the Samson riddle.
SAMSON	Good. Perhaps Dagon works with Jahveh after all.
ZOAB	Possibly. Some argue that Jahveh is the best weapon we have against your superstitious tribesmen.
SAMSON	Well, certainly, He does make things difficult from time to time. But always according to a precise plan which He never discloses.
ZOAB	We believe that all gods, like the men who invent them, have their periods of disturbance. Recently your Jahveh seems as undecided as an adolescent girl.
SAMSON	But the more neurotic He becomes the more likely are we, His people, to regain that insane puritanism which in the past has made us heroic enough to defeat history.
ZOAB	The point is that your fate demonstrates clearly the frightful revenge Jahveh takes upon his erring favourites.
SAMSON	I wouldn't rely on fear of God to frighten the Jews, if I were you. They consider it their greatest virtue.
ZOAB	We, on the other hand, study these matters comparatively. We have established that your Jahveh is a desert Wind God glorified with the attributes of an Egyptian Sun God. The eyes of his heroes

SAMSON	symbolize the heavenly orb. Their trailing hair and bristling beards, his virile rays. Oh, when will you Gentiles realize that for the Jews there is no such thing as comparative theology? There is only our own, fixed immovably.
ZOAB	Nevertheless your ordinary people are not much different from our own. They depend on their land and their animals. Sympathetic magic is as irresistible to them as it is to our own peasants. When we put out your orbs, cut off your rays, we deprived your god of his potency so far as they are concerned. It is standard primitive logic.
SAMSON	In dealing with Jews, reason will get you nowhere.
ZOAB	I agree it is all very elementary, but our long practice in the business has shown us that it always goes down well with the general public. Your blindness has gelded your people.
SAMSON	So you use Samson's decline to make Jewish hopes a laughing stock in Gaza.
ZOAB	(*sniggers*) Well, you don't have to be Jewish to enjoy Jewish jokes.
SAMSON	Samson is a very tired joke. As my mother knows quite surely, I betrayed my destiny and was punished because I went with a gentile girl. Now, please, I beg of you – do the same and let me rest.
ZOAB	Very well. (*He is about to start on the* GIRL.) You know it's strange that the special relationship you Jewish heroes are alleged to have with Jahveh, fails to restore you.
SAMSON	(*sighs*) True. No other people in history has managed to convince the world that it has a special relationship with a supreme being, and yet I feel so tired.
ZOAB	Wine and women restore man's spirit temporarily. This wine is especially strong. Why bother with your principles now? Take a glass.
SAMSON	I tried it once. It gives me heartburn.

ZOAB
: Then take this woman. It may do you good.

SAMSON
: My desire lies with my hair in a stuffed pillow under the head of a magnificent courtesan, who sleeps, I do not doubt, extremely well.

ZOAB
: And you seriously maintain that all your fabulous strength supports her head?

SAMSON
: I know it sounds as scientifically unlikely as the story of my birth. You know that fable of course.

ZOAB
: Indeed. Like all Jewish heroes, you were conceived in extraordinary circumstances. These fables get more extreme every century. Eventually your people will produce a messianic hero out of a virgin by an insubstantial spirit.

SAMSON
: (*laughs shortly*) Not even the Jews would swallow that. As for me, I was conceived in a field after a visitation from an Angel who looked much like a randy Philistine squire out for an afternoon's ride.

ZOAB
: It is possible. Our aristocracy have an insatiable fancy for Jewish girls.

SAMSON
: If I am half a Philistine, how could I ever have been a perfect working instrument for Jahveh? You know how exclusive my God and people are.

ZOAB
: Hmmmm. On the other hand, if you were half Philistine, Jahveh would know it, and if you were an imperfect instrument for Him, why should He use you for this obscure demonstration?

SAMSON
: The demonstration has failed, has it not?

ZOAB
: Most certainly.

SAMSON
: And Jahveh always knows percisely what is going to happen?

ZOAB
: So your Priests maintain. Although to us it seems absurd to give one's god such total power.

SAMSON
: It follows then that Jahveh does not want, and never has wanted, the Samson riddle to be unravelled. My story is yet another tragicomic Jewish tale with a sad ending. We have a lot of them.

ZOAB
: Good. Perhaps I may summarize. Your theory is

111

	that Jahveh gave you this incredible strength knowing that you were an imperfect vessel to contain it and that the entire demonstration would be futile and end in ignominious failure.
SAMSON	(*sighs*) That's my God.
ZOAB	But what is the profit in this?
SAMSON	We are not a trading people like you Philistines. We are a simple, agricultural, territorially-bound federation of tribes united by ten laws, which we break frequently, in the secure belief that we are the nominated protestants of an unseeable, unknowable, all-powerful God, who has reserved for us some special purpose in his quite understandable scheme of things.
ZOAB	From a merely human point of view, Samson, it is a most unsatisfactory position.
SAMSON	(*wearily*) As a mere human, Priest, I agree with you. Please now, I beg of you, service this child before she wakes and proclaims to the world my impotence. (ZOAB *kneels down to the* GIRL. *She stirs. He looks up at* SAMSON.)
ZOAB	By the way. Does it occur to you –?
SAMSON	(*irritably*) What? What?
ZOAB	She –
SAMSON	This girl?
ZOAB	No – Delilah – this girl – woman – the Harlot herself.
SAMSON	Well?
ZOAB	Make us their instruments.
SAMSON	They do. She did.
ZOAB	Well then, let me ask you one final question.
SAMSON	Ask for God's sake!
ZOAB	How could she do that against the intention of Jahveh?
SAMSON	Hmmmm. So?
ZOAB	Might she not be his instrument?
SAMSON	She might. And then?
ZOAB	(*excited at his discovery*) In which case is he not for us, for the Philistines – another guise of the Philistine god – is that not possible?

SAMSON   (*wryly*) Why not? Bless the name of the All-Possible and get on with the task in hand. (ZOAB *arranges the* GIRL'S *legs.*)
ZOAB   Yes, indeed – a most exciting thought. Thank you, sir, for a truly stimulating discussion. (*He sighs and get down to the sacred business in hand.*)

SCENE 3   TEMPLE OF DAGON

A highly dignified elderly PRIEST sits in a throne-like chair, and on a bench near him are two distinguished middle-aged executive PRIESTS. One of them reads from a tablet in his hand.

2ND PRIEST	(*reading*) 'The convocation of Brides of Dagon –'
OLD PRIEST	(*irritably*) Does that mean the entire thousand stupid girls this Jewish eunuch is alleged to have fertilized?
2ND PRIEST	That is so, your Reverence. It should make a most impressive sight.
OLD PRIEST	But, surely, it isn't necessary to have all these catawauling female idiots in the Temple at the same time. You know what excesses of hysteria these nubile girls are prone to.
2ND PRIEST	We agree, Reverence. It is not a situation we look forward to, but we all feel it necessary to make a concrete demonstration of the extent to which the alleged power of this (*he giggles*) Jewish eunuch, as you so wittily put it, has been assimilated into our Society.
1ST PRIEST	Our thinking, Reverence, is that the primitive strength so admired by our over-civilized people should be seen to re-enter our own socio-religious complex.
OLD PRIEST	(*sighs*) Our Order is becoming so sharp-minded it will cut us to pieces.
1ST PRIEST	(*gently*) We assure you, Reverence, that this entire occasion has been planned with great care.
2ND PRIEST	We are certain it will produce the desired results. (*He returns to the tablet in his hand and continues reading.*) So – 'The entire convocation of Brides of Dagon intone, "We have taken his strength into our wombs."'
OLD PRIEST	(*distastefully*) Must we be so particular?

1ST PRIEST	(*hurriedly*) In any case, Reverence, we needn't bother you with the details. The ritual will conclude with the entrance of the Great Harlot herself.
2ND PRIEST	The Man of Dan, dressed as Our Lord Dagon, will be led forward to meet her. And then –
OLD PRIEST	Yes. Yes. Most theatrical, unspeakably vulgar, and certain to please the public.
1ST PRIEST	We expect at least 2,000 witnesses of the ritual.
2ND PRIEST	Representatives of all our leading families will be there.
OLD PRIEST	It will be an occasion of unforgettable brilliance, a new ritual of historic significance. (*sighs*) Bless Dagon that my age and reverence save me from appearing on such occasions. (*He signs the tablet. The light dims on him as the* TWO PRIESTS *walk forward.*)
2ND PRIEST	I thought he'd be much more trouble.
1ST PRIEST	He's very conservative. But he knows very well that the Order must develop with the times. It's just that he prefers to ignore the details.
2ND PRIEST	I must say I think it's going to be an absolutely divine spectacle. I mean when you think of what the protagonists have been to one another –
1ST PRIEST	I do think sometimes that you are altogether too involved in theatricals and tend to neglect the ideology.
2ND PRIEST	Well, after all, it is my job to arrange these things. I must say one gets very little credit in the Order for being creative. Everything is so political these days. Or even worse, financial.
1ST PRIEST	Well, dear friend, your creativity *is* somewhat expensive.
2ND PRIEST	I'm just so delighted that I haven't had to take some ghastly rich old bag for the Great Harlot. At least Delilah is excellent casting.
1ST PRIEST	(*drily*) And half a million in silver should at least cover the cost of your enchanting costumes.

SCENE 4 THE PRISON HOUSE IN GAZA

A light reveals a gigantic terrifying figure between two columns. . . . When the lights are full on they reveal the 2ND PRIEST, assisted by THREE GIRLS costuming SAMSON (dressed as Dagon). From the Temple above sounds of a huge crowd.

2ND PRIEST   Just a moment, dear. (*He studies the costume.*) Yes. Not bad. Although I know we're going to have trouble with the fish-tail. Where is the fish-tail anyway?

GIRL   It's not finished yet.

2ND PRIEST   It's impossible. Even a professional would need some rehearsal with that contraption. And what have I got here? A blind amateur. (*Increasing sounds of crowd from above.*) Oh, listen to them! There just isn't time. They're going to have to manage without the fish-tail. (TWO PRIESTS *enter hurriedly carrying a fish-tail.*) No. No. No. It's quite useless now. There's no time to rehearse it. Take it back. (*The* TWO PRIESTS *run off with the fish-tail.*) You two girls come with me. We'd better see how the Harlot's getting on. (DELILAH *enters dressed fantastically as the Great Harlot.*) Oh! I see you're getting on very well.

DELILAH   Leave us. (*The masked head of* SAMSON *moves at the sound of her voice. The sound of the crowd from above grows louder.*)

2ND PRIEST   There really isn't very much time. We've got –

DELILAH   Leave us, I say.

2ND PRIEST   (*petulantly*) Oh! come on, girls. (*He exits followed by two of the* GIRLS. *The third* GIRL *is adjusting* SAMSON'S *costume with great absorption and does not notice the rest leave.* DELILAH *approaches and kicks the* GIRL.)

DELILAH   (*with cold command*) Get out, you little bitch!

GIRL	I – I am only doing my work, lady.
DELILAH	(*viciously*) Go do it with some diseased beggar, you gutter scut! (SAMSON *takes off his mask*.)
GIRL	(*uncertainly*) Shall I come back again later, Sir?
DELILAH	(*quietly*) Do so and I will have you split through the middle.
GIRL	Oh! (*She runs off terrified. As* SAMSON *walks forward from between the two columns* DELILAH *sees his blind face clearly for the first time and is appalled*.)
DELILAH	Your eyes!
SAMSON	(*mildly*) You were hard on the girl. She's only training to be another Delilah.
DELILAH	You stud! You Samson of little girls. Oh damn, damn and damn you!
SAMSON	You have.
DELILAH	I had it in mind to say as I saw your face 'Softly awakes my heart.'
SAMSON	A trite phrase which will never serve to remember us.
DELILAH	(*intensely*) I remember every colour in the multiple rainbow of our love.
SAMSON	Oh, no!
DELILAH	(*dramatically*) The ever changing memory obscures the sun and illuminates the night, and there is no time left for me but a time that is past.
SAMSON	An unearned income and a tragic affair have made you into a bad lady poet.
DELILAH	(*indignantly*) Do you remember nothing of our love?
SAMSON	I remember something.
DELILAH	What? Tell me?
SAMSON	I remember a certain posture of your buttocks and the whale-bone resilience of your spine. (*He stumbles as he tries again to move forward.* DELILAH *takes his arm*.)
DELILAH	Here.
SAMSON	Your hand.
DELILAH	You remember it?

SAMSON	Blindness exaggerates touch.
DELILAH	My touch was always sure upon you. Ah, that was love, love.
SAMSON	What had love to do with you except in a purely professional capacity?
DELILAH	Because I am no amateur, I take it seriously.
SAMSON	A million pieces of silver, they say.
DELILAH	Every woman longs for security.
SAMSON	Exactly. Love has a price.
DELILAH	Security is so costly.
SAMSON	Well, that's the price of love. I think that only seducers and ex-lovers ever talk of love.
DELILAH	What happened between us had the beauty of a great myth and will be remembered so.
SAMSON	Very likely. People only remember violent follies and immoderate revenges.
DELILAH	You did what few men have ever done.
SAMSON	I led men forward and found they were not following.
DELILAH	Oh, forget your unimportant military career. Your distinction is that you proved the existence of love for women.
SAMSON	So, I will comfort myself that a woman knows she has been truly loved.
DELILAH	What an unforgettable moment! As I loved you with one hand and cut your hair with the other, how hopeful I was that at last you had told me the truth, that destiny had chosen me to be the woman for whom a man would give all. If only I could make you understand what it means to a woman, who has all her life seen the promises of men explode like detumescent bubbles, to find the reality at last.
SAMSON	So, while I breathed out to you the secret of the world you were conducting some capricious female experiment.
DELILAH	I had to know. But, now, let all that be forgotten.
SAMSON	Not so easy. I have the darkness to remind me.

	(DELILAH *stares into his face for a moment. She strokes his hair and face.*)
DELILAH	Your head is still magnificent but refined somehow. I liked your hair short. It made you look boyish and vulnerable. Now it has grown again.
SAMSON	(*sighs*) Time to collect the dividend on your carefully invested million. Mock me.
DELILAH	(*genuinely hurt*) But I love you, my heart. I long for you, my lion. I ache and rave for you. My loins cry out for you. I am a vacuum without my Samson. (SAMSON *pulls away from her.*)
SAMSON	This is too female to be believed. (DELILAH *pursues him.*)
DELILAH	But that's what I am. Female is my nature.
SAMSON	Did you have some notion to get this vacuum which your nature abhors, filled?
DELILAH	Don't be bitter. It makes you crude.
SAMSON	Am I to grind daily for the Philistines and on the Sabbath tread Delilah's mill?
DELILAH	I don't wish to talk to you when you're in that mood.
SAMSON	Shall I be a bull six days a week and on the seventh your stallion?
DELILAH	Well, it's better than nothing. Listen to me, my dear. After the Great Harlot is married to the Lord Dagon in his Bull of the Sun manifestation –
SAMSON	What is this nonsense?
DELILAH	They're preparing you for the ceremony. I have bought the privilege of being the Great Harlot.
SAMSON	But what truly Great Harlot pays?
DELILAH	Be witty at my expense if you will. Pride is an impractical vanity women tolerate in men. I have none of it. So, listen. After this ritual marriage I can see no logical reason why we should not dwell together. We could make this Temple quite comfortable. (*There is increasing sound from the impatient crowd above.*) They're becoming impatient for us.
SAMSON	The building shakes under the feet of our wedding guests. (*he smiles*) Who will ever believe

	that Delilah sacrificed her love for security and her fortune for marriage?
DELILAH	(*impatiently*) Any woman would. No more talk, love. Come, love me and then let us to our wedding.
SAMSON	I see how it is with women. They want everything.
DELILAH	That's not fair. It's simply that we need as much as we can get. (*urgently*) Come to me. (*The ancient masonry of the Temple groans under the weight of the crowd above.*) Why do you wait?
SAMSON	I am studying the conclusion of my silly story. Is it that I, a general without an army, became an impotent fertility god in order to end a blind and therefore perfect husband?
DELILAH	The world is falling about us and you use the excuse of a simple accident to become an intellectual. It is something you were never very good at, brave heart. Come to me and I will cure you. (*The sound of the building groaning.* SAMSON *still hesitates.* DELILAH *puts her arms about him.*) Lie down. Be passive. We are part of it.
SAMSON	But what is it?
DELILAH	The riddle which is its own answer. Love me. (*The sound of the groaning masonry becomes very loud.*)
SAMSON	What is that thunder? Is it an answer?
DELILAH	Forget the question. We only truly follow God's will when we forget about God. (*There is a great sound of crying and shouting from above and tremendous thunderous sound as the Temple collapses... In the sudden flashes of lightning-like strobe-lighting, the tableau of* SAMSON *and* DELILAH *together... There is, of course, no prop masonry. The action is mimed.* BLACK OUT. *Dead silence for five seconds*).

SCENE 5   MANOAH'S HOUSE

MANOAH, the SCRIBE and SAMSON'S MOTHER.

MOTHER	(*ecstatic*) 'And Samson said unto the lad that held him by the hand....'
SCRIBE	(*aside to* MANOAH) He was found in her arms.
MANOAH	(*aside*) Shush!
MOTHER	'He said, "Suffer me that I may feel the pillars whereupon the house standeth that I may lean upon them."'
SCRIBE	All the Lords and the Priestesses were on the roof. Above three thousand men and women. It was an old building. It collapsed. That's history.
MANOAH	Can history argue with people who have intimate contact with angels? Take it down.
MOTHER	'And Samson called unto the Lord and said, "Oh Lord God, remember me I pray thee and strengthen me I pray thee. Only this once, oh God, that I may be at once avenged of the Philistines for my two eyes."'
SCRIBE	After this it will be war with the Philistines to the end of time. You know that, don't you?
MANOAH	Maybe that's what He wants.
MOTHER	'And Samson said, "Let me die with the Philistines."'
SCRIBE	Shall I take it down?
MANOAH	(*wearily*) Take it down, take it down. (*The* SCRIBE *writes as we fade out*...)
MOTHER	'So the dead which he slew at his death were more than they which he slew in his life.' (*She sighs with deep satisfaction*...)
SCRIBE	It is written. Shall I read it back?
MANOAH	Read it back.

SCRIBE   (*reads*) 'The Story of Samson. And the children of Israel did evil again in the sight of the Lord; and the Lord delivered them into the hands of the Philistines forty years. And there was a certain man of Zorek, of the family of the Danites, whose name was Manoah; and his wife was barren... (*The curtain falls slowly.*)

END ACT THREE